About the Author

Maxwell lives in New York City with his wife, Suzana. They resided in Europe during the pandemic for most of 2020, spending time with their three children. Maxwell continues to practice corporate law in New York City, having started his own practice in 2012. Maxwell sees his children on a regular basis and his youngest, Dori, is planning on pursuing her university studies in New York City. He loves life and is grateful for every breath of it.

WITHIN

A Memoir

This memoir is dedicated to my three beautiful children.

I want to thank my loving wife, Suzana, and my cousin Michelle for their support and input on this memoir.

Maxwell T. Dylan

WITHIN

A Memoir

Vanguard Press

A CIP catalogue record for this title is
available from the British Library.

ISBN 978-1-80016-535-9

Vanguard Press is an imprint of
Pegasus Elliot Mackenzie Publishers Ltd.
www.pegasuspublishers.com

First Published in 2023

Vanguard Press
Sheraton House Castle Park
Cambridge England
Printed & Bound in Great Britain

Contents

"For the secret of human existence lies not only in living, but in knowing what to live for."
Fyodor Dostoevsky

Night

That incessant night. I hate darkness. As dusk falls, darkness slowly closing in, I feel my mind and body change. A sense of fear, a sense of trepidation, a driving pain takes over my brain and makes its way, ever so nefariously, to my stomach and on to my extremities.

The race starts. I sleep alone, though there is no real sleep. A nagging in the mind, body and soul permeates my being, my essence—an intruder that enters the room unannounced and uninvited, ill-defined but real, certain. Carefully orchestrating my mind, it starts slow and begins to race without warning, invading my being with thoughts and feelings that fuel the sleepless night.

Darkness rocks me to sleep.

I wonder if this is it. Lost in darkness, flickers in the mind that subside then roar again, like a roller coaster. Out of my control. A rapid-fire download of my life: broken pieces, some words, other visions, random and fast.

A furtive glance at the clock, time moving ever so slowly. I wonder if there will be a sun to greet my tired being. A prayer—or rather a plea to the divine, divine will and justice; lost children, parents, a sister departed, friends gone, me alone, vanquished, supine in blackness.

Silence it! I say to myself. Please silence it. Leave my soul, my heart, my mind.

PART I

THE FAREWELL

My mother said to me not long after my younger sister died when I was seventeen years old, "Don't expect things in life, you will only be disappointed."

My French wife was finished with her experiment of living in New York. She wanted so much so fast, her expectations unfulfilled. She was a prisoner in the life she no longer desired, the life that was no longer there, and I had no choice but to let her out of her confinement and return to Paris. I could have said no, and I did say no following our separation in 2007, and the green garbage bags full of my clothing were shoved my way, and I carried the mess to the corner and dumped my life into a city rubbish bin and kept moving along the avenue sixteen blocks north to my new apartment.

I came to my former home to say goodbye to my three children on February 4, 2011. I remember that night with disturbing clarity.

~

Her boyfriend lived with her; his name was Adam and he was thin with long hair and he was a painter. He was much younger than her and she, my ex-wife, wanted to marry him. He killed himself on May 22, 2009, and I believe his suicide was the beginning of the end for me.

His lifeless body was brought to New York Hospital on a beautiful spring morning and my middle daughter was there too, getting some blood work done. The doctor wanted to make sure there was no infection since she had hurt her ankle badly.

I arrived and saw lots of doctors, nurses, administrative staff running around the place. I was instructed to go to the nurses' station, where the nurse told me my daughter, Amara, was behind the thin blue curtain. I turned and drew back the blue sheet and there she was, peering up at me from the bed, anxious.

Her mom was seated on the other side of the bed and looked up as I entered. She gave me a quick, "Hi," and went right back to her texting.

I stroked the long tousles of my daughter's brown hair and said, "Amara, don't worry, baby." And I told her, bending to kiss her on the cheek, "This is nothing. It's a simple blood test, nothing."

"I'm scared, Papa. What if something is wrong?"

I gave her a reassuring smile. "Do you know how many blood tests I've had?"

"No," she said in a tiny voice.

"Too many to count. You're going to be just fine. Don't be scared, okay?"

"Okay… but…"

"But what?"

"What if they find something bad?"

"Honey, stop. This is nothing. You hurt your ankle. They're just making sure you have no infection. It's routine stuff, that's all."

"I know but…"

"Relax. I'm here. All is good."

"Okay…"

And I saw Collette's face suddenly change. She turned white as a sheet. "Collette, is there a problem?" I said.

"Adam was in some type of an accident," she nervously replied, her voice choked with emotion.

"A bike accident?" I knew he was an avid bike rider.

She shook her head. "I don't know." Her texting grew faster and almost frantic.

"I'm sure he'll be fine." I turned back to Amara and she was sniffling. "Everything will be okay. And I added, "We'll be leaving shortly."

Collette got up abruptly and went to greet some people who had just arrived. They stepped past the curtain, and I heard inaudible voices. And then a horrifying shriek.

Amara's sniffles turned into sobs. I managed to calm her quickly and ran into the hallway and I saw two police officers and two other men trying to calm Collette.

"Can you please tell me what's going on?" I asked one of the men.

He turned. "Who are you?"

I shook my head, trying to collect my thoughts. "Collette is my ex-wife. What's going on?"

The man sighed. "Her boyfriend was found in the basement of our art gallery. I'm sorry, but he hanged himself."

"What the fuck! What happened?"

He explained that he and the other man owned the gallery, but he refused to go into detail about Adam. "You need to speak to the police." And then he gestured at the two New York cops, who were talking with some administration people.

They wouldn't say much either, but I learned that Adam had been brought to this same hospital.

I spent a few hours with Amara, trying to keep her calm and reassured while Collette was called upon to identify the body. When she returned, we all left the hospital. Collette was in shock, and I could feel the tight, airless space around her. I was worried about her.

"Collette, let me take you home, please. I'll take care of the kids, okay?"

"No, I will be fine."

I persisted but got nowhere. I touched her arm and said, "Please call me if you need anything. I'm here for you."

She did not respond. I hugged Amara. And then I turned to hug Collette, but she pulled away from me. I stood there as they walked down York Avenue toward the house.

I walked the ten blocks home to my apartment and I was out of my body and trying in vain to comprehend what had just occurred. I knew that Adam had attempted suicide years earlier. I felt horrible for him. I thought of the kids and Collette and the emotional damage that would forever be a part of their lives. And I thought of the finality of it all. No farewells, no goodbyes, no warning signs—just a man who left home in the morning, resolute in his impending violent departure. And I thought, *How brutally astounding.*

~

My charge that night arrives. I am in my office and it is dark since the light is off. I sit and stare into blackness, the door closed. I wait. I am anxious, my hands shake. I open my credenza. There, I see a bottle of vodka. I stole it from the firm Christmas party. I pour a large amount of it into a stained paper coffee cup. I gulp it down. I look at my phone. It is 5:30pm. Time to go. I walk to the bathroom and stare into the mirror. My face is gray. I take an elevator eleven floors down to the lobby and exit the building and make my way toward the house where my kids are, now home and back from school, their last day. I am cold and shaking.

I know they'd had one of the hardest days, especially my son, Gabriel, and Amara, who were saying their final goodbyes to their friends. Gabriel started a new school that he was proud of.

And all of them waiting to say goodbye and vanish into the sky.

The subway ride from my midtown law office to the house is a blur. My heart is pounding, and I am nauseous. I press my head against the cold subway window to avoid eye contact.

I exit the subway and climb up the dirty, wet stairs and hit the crooked sidewalk where I am met by multitudes of people walking, all heads pointed at the concrete. All faceless dark figures. All of them hunched over and freezing and pushing against blasts of arctic air rushing down and through the city and the tall buildings, blowing harder gusts at them. And all of it feels like a raging shark crushing my bones and tearing my skin.

When I arrive and open the black door with my old key, there I am, face to face with it all. The winding staircase is in front of me, narrow and steep, flaunting its dirty gray coat of carpet. The glossy black banister stares at me blankly and the kids' jackets hang in the entrance haphazardly. They have a sad look and I stroke them all, burying my face in those little sleeves and saying goodbye.

On top of the hall table stands a black and white photo taken of me and Collette at the altar during our marriage ceremony. It is the only picture left of me in the house, all other traces thrown out.

Climbing the winding stairs brings me back to the day my former wife called all the kids upstairs to deliver the news that we were parting.

It was a Saturday morning. I was sitting on the white sofa and Amara was slumped into the linen fabric a few feet away in her pajamas. Gabriel stood motionless by the window and Dori was aimlessly crawling.

Collette ascended the stairs to the third floor and stood by an antique French credenza. "Your father and I are going to part, since there is too much tension," she said without preamble.

Gabriel was the first to respond. "I don't understand. Does this mean we are not a family anymore? What do you mean by tension?"

"Your father and I cannot live together."

He started trembling. "But I don't understand. What does this mean? Are you breaking up?"

"Yes… We are no longer going to be together."

"But why?"

She issued a somber sigh. "I don't know. It's hard to explain, but this is what's going to happen."

"Now?"

"Yes, soon."

I was mute and I began to cry as I stared at my son. I wanted this to stop.

Amara lunged onto my lap. "I'm going with Papa!"

And I envied her strength and I felt that something was left unsaid. She calmly told the kids over her shoulder as she disappeared down the stairs, "Come down for breakfast." We were silent.

I push those thoughts away now as I ascend the stairs to see Amara. She is playing in the bathtub. She is eight years old, and I am sure that she does not comprehend the permanence of all this.

I am disturbed and cannot comprehend as I climb those stairs, the enormity of it all, knowing that my children are leaving for another country, culture, language, time-zone. *And how horrible that is*, I think. And I question whether I can survive this nightmare and I am alone and in shock but keep moving.

I need to pull the strength that I know resides in me and deal with this awful moment. I have no choice, and I think the more resilience I can muster against this terrible situation the better my children will be. I keep thinking about their confusion and sadness and my role as a father to reduce those horrible feelings.

She greets me with a big smile as she rolls around in the water like a delicate little fish. "Hi, Papa!"

I sit there in the corner, close to her, and watch her play. I think of so many moments with her as I absorb her delicate, young frame, trying to soak up every second. I try to photograph her with my eyes. I remember her as a newborn being bathed in that same bathtub.

Amara was born on September 22, 2001, eleven days after the attacks. We have just moved into our new brownstone. She was so cute, and with two kids, I had a sense of a new beginning. I would often read children's books to her as she slapped the bathwater, trying to grasp the toys that floated by. She loved being pushed around in the bath and laughed when I would tip her little shell seat. She always had a big smile. She never wanted to leave the water. As she got older, she hated having her hair brushed, as it was thick, long, and full of tangles.

Now, as I sit there, I do not know what to say to her. We are so close and yet I have no words. I am consumed with sadness.

In her innocence, she broaches the subject with a simple, straightforward question: "How long are we going to France for, and when are you coming over to stay?"

That question catches me off guard, and I sidestep it by grabbing one of the floating rubber toys and using it to tickle her ribs. She giggles.

I get her out of the bathtub, dry her off, comb her hair, and put her pajamas on. "I love you so much. You know that?"

She looks at me quizzically. "Yeah, Papa, I love you too. So, when are you coming to France?"

I look up at the ceiling in a desperate attempt to shield her from my tears. I am lost, frozen, trying to regain some composure.

"Baby, I will be there soon," I said at last. "In a few months."

"For good, right? Where are you going to live?"

I wasn't being truthful with her, and that was awful. But I continue the deception. "I don't know yet. I must do some things here. I'll be there soon."

Our eyes meet, and I see that she is trying to process my cryptic, evasive responses. "When?"

I look into her big brown eyes and say, "Are you excited to go to France... See your cousins?"

"No... I mean, yes and no." Her tiny shoulders moved in a shrug. "I have friends here."

"I know you do."

"I don't want to go."

"Why not?"

"I don't know. It's weird you are staying here."

I stand up in this small, airless bathroom, the sweat now gathering on my face. I grab a hand towel and wipe my brow. "I have to stay here for now, but then I'll come... Okay?"

"When?" She was being persistent and had every right to be. That was her personality. If she felt her questions were not being answered to her satisfaction, she would just keep going until she had an answer that she desired.

And I know I can't give her one. "Soon, baby, very soon. You know I love you and I'm going to miss you so much. You know that, right?"

"Yeah, Papa." But she is not finished yet. "Papa, are we leaving because you and Mom fight all the time?"

That stunned me. I thought about all those times when I had visitation with the kids on weekends, and Amara would blurt out, usually when we were outside walking up a street, "Papa, my mom does not like you."

Gabriel would immediately step in. "Amara, shut up! That's not true!"

I knew Gabriel was trying to protect me, and I wondered what my former wife was saying to the children.

"Amara," I say to her now, "we did not fight all the time but sometimes we had differences, and that would sometimes make us angry at each other. Parents do not get along all the time."

I know she isn't buying it, but she keeps silent as I finish buttoning her pajamas.

"Okay, jams on. I'm going to see Dori, okay?"

"Okay," she said. "I'm going to watch TV."

I kiss her brown eyes, hug her, and tell her that I love her.

"Love you too." She leaves the bathroom and races upstairs to watch a show.

I sit there, drained, then go to see my youngest, Dori. She is on the floor of her bedroom with crayons and paper scattered all around her. She smiles at me when I enter and then returns to her drawing.

For a time, I sit on her bed and watch her without saying anything. She looks so cute and round, like a little ball. I want to pick her up in my arms and kiss her, but I don't' want to disturb her. She is an artist absorbed in her own creative process.

I find myself in the same situation as with Amara moments earlier. The difference is that Dori is only five years old and cannot comprehend that she is moving to France.

She was a tactile baby, and would always crawl to me, wanting to climb onto my back. She loved animation films, and together we would watch movies for hours while she lay on my back or cuddled into me, getting her position right and comfortable to watch the movie. Dori was my baby, and I could not see her any other way. She was a warm girl and very emotional, like me.

"Papa, can you scratch my back?" she asked.

"Yes, baby." I move to the floor and begin scratching her back. "So, Dori, those are very pretty drawings. You are a true artist."

"Thanks, Papa. A little harder."

"What have you been drawing?"

She holds one picture above her head. "Do you like this one? It's a pony."

"Yes, honey, it's a beautiful painting."

She puts down the paper and gives me a hug. "Papa, it's not a painting. It's a drawing."

"Oh, sorry. That's a beautiful drawing. I love ponies."

"I know."

My emotions are again ramping up and taking control of my mind. This is becoming too much for me and I want to disappear.

"Papa, why are you crying?" she asked.

"I just got something in my eye." Brushing away the tears, I stand and move across to the window and I stare out at the backyard, trying to calm myself. I do not want her to see me like this.

"Papa, what are you doing?" she exclaims.

"Nothing, baby. Just looking at the backyard."

"It's dark. You can't see anything."

I turn and walk back over to sit on the floor next to her. She is back to her drawings.

"Hey, can I get a real hug?" I asked.

"I gave you one already."

"I know, but how about a big one, you and me?"

"Okay."

I cannot let go of her. I start to cry again, silently. This time I manage to hide my tears from her. I keep my face hidden, pressing it against her softly.

I collect myself, as best I can, and get to my feet. "Baby, I love you. Now I need to see Gabriel."

"Why?"

"Just to talk for a while."

"Okay." She eyes her latest creation critically.

"I love you."

She looks up at me. "Papa, you keep saying that. I know you do."

As I leave her bedroom, I find the Nanny standing nervously in the hallway. She informs me that the kids' dinner is ready, and that Collette would be home shortly.

I nod and keep moving, feeling numb as I ascend another flight of stairs. That all-too-familiar smell of the third-floor hits me at once. It is a musty smell, not pungent, but soothing. The ceiling is almost twenty-five feet high, dominated by a large, angled glass structure, framed in thick gray steel, pointing directly at the sky.

This entire floor was our playroom, and it evoked in me so many fond memories. It was a place where we all spent a lot of time hanging out and messing around with all kinds of toys or watching movies and reading together. Though it was a large room, it always felt intimate to me.

But on this dreadful night, this room is no longer intimate. It has morphed into a cold, depressing place, unrecognizable. The memories sucked right out of this sanctuary that was once upon a time ours to share. It hits me hard in my gut as I look around and see flickers of our past, our precious times spent together as a family now stripped away from us for no good reason.

Gabriel sits on the white sofa, leaning forward, hunched over like he had a writhing pain in his core—this young boy, my son, whom I loved so much, now in such unrelenting pain. A father just watching, powerless to quell his suffering. How awful that felt.

His long legs are shaking rapidly, and one hand is scratching his head ferociously like he is trying to rip his hair out. His blue eyes flicker here and there, looking at everything but me. He has been crying.

And as I move closer, he begins to slowly prop his lanky frame up and his blurry blue eyes, puffy and red, finally meet mine. His stare is listless, dead.

I sit next to him at the edge of the sofa. I want to grab him and just run and I want to give him what I cannot offer and I am desperate and powerless to calm him.

"This whole thing is stupid," he said.

I hesitate for a moment, look him in the eye and say in a soft tone, "I agree with you. It's stupid."

"I have friends here. This is my home. I have no interest in going to France."

"I know." My son was smart beyond his years. Perhaps, I thought, he just might understand the dynamic that I had no control over. "Gabriel, your mom and I are not in love. I know that might sound harsh to you, since we are your parents and love is something that parents should have for each other. It did not work out that way for us. You see?"

He stares at me.

"Things don't always work out the way you want them to. Things in life can get complicated. We tried. Believe me, we did. It just never happened the way we wanted it to. Remember when your mother said there was too much tension between us, and that was why we were parting? You recall that?"

He nods, his eyes still fixed on mine.

"Well, that was her way of saying that we could not work as a married couple living together, you see? This is why all this is happening, and your mother now wants to go home to Paris."

"Yeah, but what about you? What do you want?"

"I don't want her to take you to Paris. I don't. But I see her unhappiness living in this country. It has been building up inside her for many years. I could say to her, 'No, you have to stay here.'" I drew a breath, fighting back the tears that again threatened to flow. "I could do that, my son. But I decided that it would be unfair to her. I thought that I had no right to keep her here and allow her to be unhappy."

I see from his body language that my feeble attempt to calm him has no impact on his agitated state.

I continue, though. "Gabriel, we both love you and the girls more than anything in the world. That will never change."

He remains silent, but I see he is slowly beginning to take bits and pieces of this into his mind, processing what I am saying. "Why don't you try to fix it with mom?"

"As hard as we tried, we failed to come to a place where we could understand each other and go back together. This does not mean we won't work as hard as we can to make sure your life and the girls' lives will be great. We absolutely want that as your parents. We just can't do it in the same house."

He gets up from the sofa and steps over to the window; the same window where he'd stood the day his mother told him we were parting.

I look around, thinking of the times in this very room when we had built his train and Lego sets. He loved trains. He would meticulously construct all the tracks, placing the little villagers precisely where he thought they belonged. He had a clear vision of what this train village was supposed to look like, and he was insistent on his design skills. We had so many loving moments then.

I look over at his tall, lanky frame as he stands facing the window, wanting nothing to do with me. "Gabriel, can we talk about this more?"

He remains silent, staring out the window. I hear him sniffling and periodically brushing his hand across his face.

"What's there to talk about?" he asks, his voice barely above a whisper. "I'm going, and that's it. You know that Papa, so we really have nothing to say to each other."

"I would feel the same as you if my parents were doing this, breaking up the family and taking me away from my friends. I would be mad and upset."

Nothing.

"I don't want to keep your mom in a place where she is unhappy."

He jerks and spins around. "What about us? It's all about her!"

"She wants to go back to her family, your grandparents. I know you like them. And you like Paris. Heck, how many times have we visited? We all had such a good time."

"Papa, that was vacation."

"I know, but we all have great memories from those trips. It's not a strange place, and I will be visiting a lot. I know some of your friends, and they are great. But guess what? You'll be coming back here to see me and them."

"It's not the same."

"I know. All we can do is try to make it better, and it will get better. I'll be coming to Paris a lot to see you and the girls, and you'll be coming here a lot, school breaks and summers. We're going to have a lot of fun. Then, when you get a little older, you can decide where you want to live. This is not just about your parents. You will have a say in all of this. Time goes quick, and that day will arrive soon."

He draws in a breath and releases it in a deep sigh. He seems more relaxed.

We sit in silence for a while longer. I hold his hand. He didn't object, which I see as a good sign. I finally release it and get to my feet. "I have to go. Your dinner is ready, and your mom will be home soon."

"Who cares?" he mutters.

I kiss him on the cheek and say, "I love you." While he does not directly offer any response, his eyes and demeanor seem calmer. I am happy with that. At this point I will take anything.

~

I leave feeling like I want to die, a listless, out-of-body walk, one foot in front of the other, to the corner of First Avenue, where I take a taxi and head north to retreat into my apartment where I stare into empty space.

I think of loss. And I think of my mother on the day she received a phone call from Columbia Presbyterian Hospital and was instructed by the caller to make an immediate appointment to have my little sister, Mary, begin radiation and chemotherapy for leukemia.

And I remember days following the aftermath of that awful event seeing my mother one afternoon sitting alone at our kitchen table. I was twelve years old. She sat there, her head awkwardly weighing down, her eyes heavy-lidded and mute. Tears streaming down, silent, her face motionless. I studied her from behind as she sat there at the long, dark brown kitchen table, where we would always gather for our meals. It was a place where we would talk about the events of our day and engage in conversation. My mother was now taking refuge there for a different, life-changing event.

I remember feeling helpless at that moment, since there was nothing that I could say or do that would placate her. My instincts told me that my mother was not interested in a hug or any words from me; she needed time to herself, and to be alone with her thoughts.

For a moment I think of the East River and its proximity. I don't believe that I can sustain this wreck of my existence. It is a long night, and I never knew silence could be that loud.

PART II

NEW YORK CITY

I remember asking my father where my surfboard was since I wanted to go surfing that day and he said to me, "I threw it out because it was yellowish in parts and old." That long piece of foam infill encased in resin was precious to me and it harbored all my past experiences surfing my ocean. Now, it was orphaned somewhere in a dumpster. I thought to myself, *Did any of this really exist to begin with?* And I still long for my past to come into focus. And the days as a young kid surfing those waves began to fade and I retreated from him.

I thought of Central Park as my new ocean and a place to get back to where I came from and I arrived alone and in search. Running replaced surfing and offered me aloneness and the immersion of myself in nature like my submersion into the saltiness of the sea riding my childhood plank on the rollers.

Salvator was there to greet me at the reservoir early most mornings as the sun began to wake up. "Hi, Salvator, how are you holding up today and did you walk the reservoir without me?" I always greeted him that way. He was an old man and had the most beautiful, tanned skin and blueish green eyes that flickered with amazing divine light, and he was thin and gaunt with deep crevices circling his neck. Everything about him was old except his eyes that were the same color as the tropical sea and were unconquered and cheerful.

He spoke poor English and had come from Puerto Rico many decades prior and found his home by the reservoir where he took up residence on a green bench in front of the water pump station. He carried a cane, and we walked slowly together around the loop of the reservoir most mornings. He was quiet and spoke without saying much.

Following our morning walk and my goodbye to Salvador, I started running and meditating and thinking without being disturbed and feeling my endorphins gaining on me and coursing through my veins in my new ocean. I thought of all this nature, resting in the middle of the tall buildings that would constantly change color against the morning sun. The old man and I agreed that the large buildings seemed so far from us even though they were upon us.

My favorite moments there were early morning as the sun began to rise, or in the late afternoon, at dusk. The early mornings were especially beautiful, since it was quiet, with only a few runners in the park except for Salvador.

Some late afternoons I would come by the park to drink a beer or two with him. He told me stories about Puerto Rico and his days as a young fisherman. He loved the sea and we spoke a lot about it and he learned of my youth and my surfing adventures. He surged back with stories of the days he rested in the cradle of the sea and the fish he so loved when he was young and agile, pulling into his tiny wooden craft the blue marlin and Allison tuna that he proudly conquered. We had a lot in common and we were grateful to swim together in our new ocean.

One day he asked, "Are you a big wave surfer?"

I responded, "Sometimes."

He laughed. "Where have you surfed big waves?"

I was a little caught off guard and I could see a smile crease on his face. The beer made him a little giddy. "I don't know, New Jersey."

Salvador then let out the biggest belly laugh and leaning forward on the green bench retorted, "New Jersey! Then you are not a big wave rider."

I knew he was messing with me but continued. "Why?"

"That is easy, because there are no big waves to ride in New Jersey, my friend. That's why." He continued with fiery glee pouring from his eyes. "Where I come from… My friend, now that is big waves. Outside of old San Juan there is a place called Puerta de Tierra, near Escambron Beach, where the biggest waves are as tall as some of those buildings around us." His head and hands reached for the sky and then he looked me right in the eye. "You are not a big wave man until you ride those mountains." He continued. "But, my friend, you must go there in the wintertime. That's when they come."

"Okay," I responded meekly. It was my turn now. "What about you, old man? Did you ever surf as a kid in Puerto Rico?"

He looked at me quizzically, putting both hands on his chest and leaning back on the green bench. "I am a fisherman, an old fisherman."

"Well…" I said, "Old fishermen can sometimes be surfers too."

He grinned with a slight chuckle "Yes, but I am just a fisherman. That was my life."

I said, "I know, but you could surf too."

The old man thought for a second and laughed. "Oh yes, but I did in a way."

"How?" I asked.

He then leaned into me and spoke very directly. "Well… When you fish you need to take your boat through the waves and when you come home in the dark night you must sometimes navigate the big waves and use your oar to get to shore, so that is like surfing, boat surfing. It is very dangerous and takes much skill… So maybe I am a surfer after all." He laughed again and I knew he was playing with me. "But what you must be most careful of in Puerto Rico are the tiburon. Yes, they come at night mostly and are hungry."

"Tiburon, what is that?"

"Sharks, my friend. They like fishermen because we carry on the side of our boats big fish that we caught. They don't fit in the boat, so we tie them to the side and the blood that pours from these big fish like a gigantic tuna goes right into the sea, you see, and the sharks smell that blood. They smell blood miles away and come attacking. Many times, there is nothing left of your fish when get to the shore."

He continued, proudly now. "But, my friend, I was the conqueror of tiburon. I used my oar to beat them back." I was famous for that when I was young man."

I smiled and asked, "Well maybe one day you can show me how to fish in Puerto Rico and teach me how to beat the sharks."

The old man leaned back on the green bench and spoke. "I think you should stick to surfing, my friend, and go to Puerto Rico and I can watch you conquer the big waves."

"That's a deal, Salvador. One day…"

~

New York was different when I touched its shores in 1987. My childhood was forty minutes from the city and I would think about it from time to time. The meat packing district consisted of stained cobblestone streets set obscurely at the edges of Soho and Tribeca and was dimly lit with old industrial warehouse rises and rusty old burning barrels and men swarming around the flickering glow that reached up to the sky where the stars were not visible. The men wearing bloodied white coats loaded animal parts onto trucks that came and went all day and night long.

Soho was a barren concrete landscape, and the inhabitants were primarily struggling artists who took residence in the cheap lofts. There were no restaurants or trendy stores there, just a handful of delis and an occasional dimly lit, decaying Irish watering hole.

The Lower East Side, commonly referred to as Alphabet City, was a war zone during the eighties and early nineties and was off-limits. Tompkins Square Park was home to all the drug addicts and pushers. And other areas, like Chelsea, Hell's Kitchen, and East Harlem were viewed the same way.

The feeling of anonymity in this city was alluring. I felt the sheer density of it. I was free, so I thought.

~

The Upper West Side was where I lived and I saw multiple personalities come and go. Most people arrived from all parts of the world and carried a different attitude and way of life, weaving it right into the fabric of this area that would turn on a dime within the space of a city block, going from seedy, to industrial, to chic, and to All-American. Painters, actors, intellectuals, and writers lived there.

I took an apartment with my younger brother on 83rd Street and Broadway. The apartment had two bedrooms, a large dining room and a living room, with a long foyer and glass French doors throughout. Our apartment was on the fifth floor and adorned with natural hardwood floors and moldings that lined the tall ceilings.

The shops that lined the avenues were small ethnic shops that gave me a warm sense of community and inviting smells of ethnic cooking. There was a large Hispanic population there and many bodegas served up authentic Cubano sandwiches and other exotic food from their countries. Occasionally I bought Cubano sandwiches and went to the park and the old man and I would eat lunch together. I knew many of the owners of the restaurants and they were kind and cooked some of the best cuisine I ever tasted.

I went to small theatres and a small book shop called Shakespeare & Co., which was discreetly tucked away on the corner of 82nd Street and Broadway. The shop was warm and comforting and I spent a lot of time there reading plays.

~

Zabar's market was the largest marketplace in my neighborhood. The food market was always crowded and people would come from all over the city to buy food there. Bagels, smoked fish, olives and cheeses.

When I entered the store, I was met by many shoppers of all ethnicities, racing about the store, and yelling above the unrelenting noise, a few feet deep from the counter, making their food orders and fiercely pointing at the selections they wanted.

The store aisles were cluttered and very narrow throughout the place. This created constant congestion, and on many occasions gridlock, especially among the mothers who would push their kids around in strollers. I saw people get into many arguments.

I went there on Saturdays to look at all the food. The workers were very nice and I spent most of my time with the smoked fish servers. They were mostly older men who came from parts of Eastern Europe and they could tell you anything you wanted to know about the fish. They did not let the patrons disturb their putative dominance.

Alex was my favorite purveyor, and he liked my sense of humor. He was a hard worker and knew everything there was to know about all the smoked fish he sliced.

"The fish looks excellent today," I said.

Alex looked up with a big smile. He stared at me and then, in broken English, responded, "Yes, it is my friend."

I knew, without him telling me, that I was under strict watch. He never minced his words and we got to know each other very well.

He was a nice man. He was bald and had stout, clay fingers and gigantic, clubby hands and a thick back. He was from the former Soviet empire and like many Jewish Russians landed in Israel prior to coming to the United States. Most of them went to Brooklyn, to an area called Little Odessa.

Alex invited me to his tiny apartment for dinner and then took me to a Russian café and we drank a lot of vodka. He told me about what it was like to live in Russia and I could tell he missed his home. He was lonely and enjoyed the time we spent together. I remember we spent a whole day together one Sunday and he took me to the good Russian markets in Little Odessa and had me try all sorts of Russian food. It was wonderful to be with him and I learned everything there was to know about the food. He became much younger when he spoke about his native cuisine and I felt he transported himself back to a happier time in his life.

"Let's see," I said, as I pondered the large selection. "The smoked white fish looks great today." I was proudly standing there in my pajama bottoms, my hair sticking up all over the place, and I was wearing a cheap pair of sandals with no socks and a soiled sweatshirt. I looked homeless.

He hesitated for a second, and offered bluntly, "Sure, but you must be careful, you should get something to buy. The boss is watching me and he knows you."

"Oh, don't worry. I am ready to go today. Let's give it a try." He took his thin carving knife and cut the smallest sliver of the white fish, placed it on some parchment paper and handed it over.

"Alex, thanks." I quickly gobbled it down and stared at him like a hungry puppy. I bought a little bit of fish that morning. Alex was happy.

~

I practiced law and didn't like it very much. I was feeling suffocated and I thought lawyers were not that nice. I was becoming tired of the games and rules that I was required to follow.

My job during law school, to be the person who interviewed death row inmates in the lawsuit that my law professor filed in a big courthouse, was the exception. This lawsuit was not about getting these inmates off death row; this was about pursuing deplorable conditions at the hands of the criminal system and cruel and usual punishment.

I remember heading off to Indiana State Penitentiary to interview the death row inmates about their prison conditions. I imagined guards and protection as I drove three hours in the cold and daunting Midwestern desert, wearing the same stuff I wore as a law student working for the public defender: I was clad in blue jeans, a white T-shirt, and denim coat, all cheap and disposable. I had no idea what awaited me.

I got my first glance at this old penitentiary covered in a morning mist with guards walking atop the prison fortress with guns. Towers surrounded the facility and barbed wire was everywhere and I arrived at perdition.

As I entered the prison, I was hit by a rank smell and everything was slow-moving. I went to the canteen at lunchtime and was met by fiercely loud acoustics. I looked out over the sea of inmates and heard their screams of innocence and passion and rage.

The interviewees then appeared one after another, tight handcuffs on their wrists and legs. Their security detail was serious and young and strong, carrying large guns, unholstered, and one after another escorting the doomed men to my table and guiding them to their seats and chaining the detainees to the floor. The long interviews went on for weeks.

~

I also studied acting and I liked it. I went to many of the off and off-off theatre shows. I loved to read plays and soon became friends with many of the playwrights in the city. I studied at various studios and found a home at the Lee Strasberg Theatre and Film Institute, a school for method acting.

Alex loved theatre and on his days off we would meet from time to time near his apartment in Brooklyn and spend afternoons at a local Russian café sharing our thoughts and experiences. Alex was very knowledgeable, and I remember him becoming excited, speaking about Konstantin Stanislavsky and method acting and many Russian actors and playwrights that he was passionate about. Alex spoke of the many performances he attended when he lived in Russia. He was well versed in Russian literature and knew all the great authors.

I learned a lot from Alex. He loved art and told me of the times when he was younger and hanging around Arbat Street in Moscow. All the artwork he saw on the facades of old Soviet era houses and abandoned factories and walls. He told me of this famous street that was only moments away from Red Square and that he and his friends would sometimes smoke pot and laugh from a distance at all the soldiers that were prevalent.

"My wife was a great actress. She died a long time ago," he said one day when we were outside the café. I was stunned when he told me this. I felt so bad for him and I was surprised, since he had never mentioned anyone by name from his past before. He was sad looking when he told me this.

I tried to cheer him up and replied, "Now, Alex, I truly understand where your great knowledge of the arts was forged." I saw a thin smile appear and I knew at that moment he was lighter in thought. He never mentioned her after our quick exchange.

~

The eighties and early nineties were a good time for thespians since things were more experimental and riskier in theatre. I was happy to be a part of it. I liked the social life around the craft. Everything flowed and I flowed effortlessly in that milieu. The nights were typically long and many evenings I found myself at these gatherings where well-known actors were present. I never felt out of place or that there was any sort of hierarchy in these situations. People came to talk of plays and party. I remember greeting many mornings bleary eyed, wired and content. I asked Alex to come with me to some of these late-night gatherings and he politely declined. He was satisfied with our talks and sought nothing more.

Alex tired of New York and eventually decided to move to California. He told me that the cold was always a part of his life in Russia and he wanted to experience America and the great western expanse he saw in the movies. He said, "I learned so much watching those old movie Westerns and I want to experience and see that with my own eyes before I die." I was happy for him and he left the city and traveled west, closer to his childhood dreams. We never saw each other again.

Old man, Salvador, never left the city. Our relationship only deepened over the years and I liked that.

~

I thought the city would be my protector. I was wrong.
I was tired. I fell asleep and I dreamt about a white wolf.

PART III

"IN AND OUT"

I leave our home on the morning of January 6, 2007. She states evenly at breakfast that I should rent an apartment. Her eyes are pale and I push the oatmeal away and I drink my coffee and I light up a cigarette. The kids are not present and my departure is silent.

~

I met her in a French restaurant in the city. She was attractive, young and rebellious and was always saying whatever came to her mind. I was intrigued by her; I was lost.

She was from a small town west of Paris and it was bourgeois. Versailles was close. Village streets were narrow and I saw plenty of old homes and tiny stores tucked to the side, and family-owned boutique shops selling fresh bread and pastries and meats, newspapers, magazines and cigarettes. There was a pharmacy and a small brasserie and locals gathering there for café and drink. The church stood tall in the middle of it all.

~

I walk up Third Avenue randomly appearing in the lobbies of high-rise residential buildings in search of a home. The street is calm and a few yellow cabs veer slightly my way in hopes of capturing an early morning fare. I pass familiar stores and restaurants and I am cold and I continue up the avenue and I think of my kids.

I pass New Yorkers scrambling in their running gear toward Central Park and pigeons scattering out of their way and I think of the old man. And I want to talk to him and walk with him and eat with him and speak about the sea and our new ocean and I press forward.

I call my sister to let her know and she goes to work and organizes the move. And I continue.

I see a building on 87th Street and Third Avenue that is across from a large AMC movie theatre complex where I would take the kids. It is a brown brick high rise building with a wide circular drive-through and a huge entrance with three revolving doors like those in a casino you would pull up to in Las Vegas, doormen adorned in their brown caps, brown jackets and pants with yellow-lined piping down the sides, quickly circling all around me like a pack of sharks nodding and saying hello and I enter the lobby.

The lobby is enormous and I am met by high ceilings with gaudy prominently displayed chandeliers dangling from everywhere and different colored chairs, sofas and ugly looking tables scattered throughout, and a busy colored carpet that reminded me of some Marriot hotel.

And then the on-site broker appears and is racing across the vast lobby, leaning forward, her long stringy bleached blond hair floating up on each side of her thin, gaunt face from the gusts of wind that would blow through the area like a wind tunnel. She has deep black crevices under her eyes like a small raccoon. She awkwardly manages, with a clipboard in one hand, to quickly extend her other hand, offering me a firm handshake and a quick introduction. Without me saying a word, she tells me that a two-bedroom apartment on the tenth floor had just been renovated and is available for immediate occupancy. She looks anxious to get a closing done that day. Her breath reeks of coffee and she looks beat.

We arrive at the floor and she is fumbling for the keys to the apartment. The hallway matched the carpeting and wallpaper in the lobby. She manages with her shaky hands to unlock the door and I enter the dwelling. I am met with a fresh paint smell right away. It is a long, bare, symmetrical apartment, newly boarded fabricated shiny wooden flooring throughout, bright white walls and ceilings that are typical in the high rise buildings that line Third Avenue. The apartment has a lot of big windows and is directly across from the 86th street subway station and the sunlight streams brightly into every room.

Moving quickly through the place I enter the kitchen, which has an L-shaped stone granite floor design, new appliances with a big window that faces west toward the park. The broker is incessantly trying to focus my attention on the new appliances. She believes it is a huge selling point. "The refrigerator is sub-zero. Hard to find. And look, see the stove, all stainless steel. Nice, right?" I agree and keep moving through the place as she tags along behind me with her clipboard in hand.

I walk toward the window in the living room and look out at an old grimy water tank on the roof opposite. That old tank triggers memories of living on the West Side so many years prior where they were a fixture on the tops of most pre-war buildings. And I think of Alex and think about his dreams of the west and whether they came true the way he wanted and I long for a conversation with him in that Russian café.

I want to go back to my bookstore and I want to perform on a stage and eat smoked fish, and drink vodka with Alex; I want no part of this.

I continue to the master bedroom and mentally measure the space for a big bed and crib for Dori. I continue to another room off the kitchen and perform the same mental measurement for my other two kids.

As I walk through the place I can hear the faint sound of traffic on the avenue and occasionally the hissing sound of a transit bus coming to a stop at the bus station which is on the corner right below the building. I am disturbed by it all and I am gasping for air. I open the window and stick my head out and stare toward the park and silently ask the old man to come.

"So, what do you think?" the broker says. She is hustling to get the place rented.

"I like it, I really do. I am thinking about the space for my three kids, you know, enough room for them to play and run around."

She is quick to respond. "That's important. I have two kids myself and completely understand." She keeps insisting that the apartment was seen by several people already and would probably go that day. "But," she says, "it's yours, of course, if you take it now."

I ask her when I could move in.

"Now," she responds abruptly.

"That's great. It works, it really does. I'll take it now." I can tell she is stunned.

"Wonderful. Trust me." She is fumbling with her clipboard, with nervous excitement about my quick decision. "You will be so happy here. And so close to the subway and park."

I nod in agreement.

I have all the necessary paperwork with me and take the place right away. The broker, I believe, sort of got what was happening without me saying a word. I sign everything, cut the checks, and leave for my sister's apartment a short distance away. We get the place set up the same day and I am tired. And sad.

~

Collette was *bourgeoisie* and I was suffocating under the weight of the inflexible rules that I was obligated to abide by. And the distance. And the protocols prevailing, and a guessing game as to what piece of tableware I was required to use at dinner, and secretly waiting for the first person at the table to make a move and then quietly following, undetected. And I did not belong.

My mother pulled no punches and she was polite and brutally honest. She was observant and well-researched and decisive; I learned that as a thirteen-year-old kid following her around and watching her moves with doctors who were caring for my sister. She knew what Mary needed despite the doctor's instructions on procedures and certain medications that Mary was required to take. At the time, many of these cancer medications were considered pioneering drugs that led to unanticipated side effects that could be very harmful. My mother understood that and would calibrate the doses based upon her own feelings and observations concerning her daughter, putting aside the doctor's advice. And she was correct all the time. She knew Mary better than anyone and was confident in her decisions.

My mother and I spent a lot of time together during Mary's illness. We became very close through this ordeal. One thing that has stuck with me was how strong and resilient my mom was throughout Mary's cancer. It was remarkable to watch her strength and I was so proud of her.

~

I remember my mother's instincts were on fire when she arrived in the central part of France on July 24, 1996, a few days before the wedding at the Chateau. It was this humongous 'in-the-family' structure and needed care.

She eyed the murky pond in front of the huge and decaying structure in the central mountains of France resting on top of a large hill. And she saw the green algae and large plants that protruded from the dark, dense water and into the air pointing directly at the summer sky.

And she felt the heat of the summer and silently viewed the elderly French ladies spending hours picking vegetables from the garden and doing laundry and other tasks. And the flies swarming.

And she smelt the *bourgeoisie*. She struck gently and truthfully, and I ignored her and she was my teacher.

And on the morning of the wedding, we met and I was going to run. And she searched without influencing and asked without expecting and she sat on her bed changing her leg prosthetic. And she said softly, "Maxwell, how are you?"

I sensed a follow-up question was coming and I knew the cadences that I had heard as a kid. And I responded knowing that voice and understanding her question meant something else. "Fine, Mom," I said.

And she thought and continued. "Well, good, are you happy?" she asked.

And I said, "Yes." And I knew.

"Okay, my dear. You know that we could make this into a vacation and return to Paris together and it would be fine."

And I looked at her and lied. "I am fine and I am happy."

She wished me a good run and I kissed her on the forehead and left.

The day came: nuptials performed, toasts raised, speeches made, and a lot of champagne and wine poured throughout the evening into the early morning for those that could make it. And it was over.

~

We began a new life as a married couple in New York City. She tried to transport her French culture with her and it did not work. She was young and naïve and I assumed she would adapt; she did not. The reality of it all came crashing down on her, the permanency of this new frontier. Our summers were spent with her family in France.

Our marriage was slipping well before we got divorced and then abruptly ended. It was 'in and out', I thought.

~

Some years passed and with two children things shifted for us. We were not a happy couple, and our lives together were full of tension and lacked joy as we struggled to manage our decaying union. And we both learned the hard way.

I remember one Saturday morning at the kitchen table where Collette's frustration toward me was certain. Nothing that I would do or say was right to her. She constantly questioned my place in it all. I was an outsider looking in, so I felt to her. And that left me struggling and lost and alone.

That morning, she appeared in the kitchen disturbed, anxious and unsettled.

She asked coldly, "What are we going to do today?"

I was caught off-guard and grappled to find a response since I had none. *Ah, here we go,* I thought to myself. "I don't know, let's take the kids to the park, maybe go to movie, you know relax, hang out."

She gave me a frustrated look and then out of nowhere said, "Maxwell, you have no friends, what are you going to do this weekend?"

I nodded in disbelief. *Not this again,* I thought. "What?" I blurted back pretending not to hear the statement that was just launched my way, praying it would vanish into the air without requiring any response. I could feel the tension building but tried to ignore it.

And she persisted, firing off another pointed question that left me confused and frustrated. "Why do you have no plans? We do nothing."

Well, I shrugged. "I have friends. I mean, who cares." I could not find any response that I thought would make this go away. So, without making eye contact I said, "Relax. We'll figure something out, plenty to do."

I knew my answer would not satisfy her. She hesitated. I knew she was not done. Or, for that matter, believed in anything I had to say on the subject.

She was correct. I was left with nothing to offer that could possibly diffuse her apparent frustration with me. My attempts to lighten this heaviness in her never took root.

I recoiled, remained silent and thought of ways to remove myself from this uncomfortable situation. My escape was always to run for the kids. I knew we were heading into awful territory, stretched out silences, wrong, confused looks toward each other, and a place where reason didn't work.

~

I was lost in my own home and I could not find a place to hide. I was in a constant state of distraction and agitated most times. I did not belong there and I saw myself slowly resign. I would wander around my home, hoping for a spot to let my mind go and relax. Reading the paper or a book was of no use. I could not concentrate. I would read a chapter of a book and not recall a word of it. I remember waiting for something to happen and was expecting her to appear and criticize me. She made me aware of what I was doing wrong. I escaped to Central Park and spent time with old man and I went on runs.

~

Sometimes during those lost moments in my home, I thought of my father and the times growing up where I would wander that big house trying to find a spot, or really hide from him. A hiding game, nervous about the impending cross-examination. *Did I marry my father,* I thought.

My father required order and she demanded it. He could be judgmental of me and others and so was she. When they were forced to listen to what I wanted to say, they would become increasingly agitated with every assertion I made, especially when we disagreed or had different opinions. And they rarely spoke *to* me, but rather at me.

~

I remember desperately wanting to remove myself from it all. I did not count. And I wanted freedom and did not know what that meant any more. And I thought of my childhood and those beautiful waves I surfed. I wanted to go back home and surf them again and ride my plank through the decay and crouch on my board and take that vertical plunge down to the base of the wave and hear the ocean roaring and chasing me from behind and me, seconds ahead, and slowly cutting across the wave and now in control and riding it down First Avenue and shifting my board with some pressure on its tail, delicately adjusting my position and veering right and traversing effortlessly across town and then straightening out this glorious ride with nature and gliding peacefully along the Hudson and making my way and hearing the noise of the massive wave breaking over my head and me protected in the barrel of this gentle giant and pointing my wax arrow straight down south to my childhood.

And being at peace with waves all around me and breaking perfectly and seeing second and third breaks crashing far off the shores. And drinking the sprays and feeling wind blowing and seeing rocketing saltwater spray shooting sky-high and wild mists peeling away from these glorious titans. And my sandy runway, huge and expansive, and the crushing nature on the water stage divinely choreographed in exquisite precision, smothering my being in the flickering blue sea.

And my nuns migrating like penguins from their beachfront convent to the shoreline to take in the water show. And my private ballet on the ocean and my nuns watching. And at dusk leaving my cathedral flogged and bloodied from the water dance.

~

Following that morning encounter, I pushed my bowl aside and got up from the table and excused myself. "Well," I sighed, "I am going to watch a movie upstairs with the kids." They were my solace. It did not last though. She would not stop. I have no idea why.

She retorted with a slight French accent as I got up from the table and headed for the stairs, "You never read to them. You don't."

"Right," I shrugged. I kept moving to the staircase as my agitation was becoming more apparent. "Wait, what was that?" I said turning back toward her. "Yes I do and why are you so upset? It is Saturday. There is lots to do in the city. We can go to the museum, or something."

Then, without addressing my statement she moved to another topic and firmly stated to me, "Amara has a birthday party to go to. You need to take her there."

"Oh," I said. "I had no idea. Fine. I'll take her."

I did my best to ignore this onslaught. I was trying to manage the situation since that was all I thought I could do. I was lost in it all.

I sighed and said, "Come on, stop this. It's Saturday, cool it."

She retreated a bit, and I ascended the stairs totally confused. I thought to myself, *Is it me or is she miserable?*

~

Weekday nights were becoming increasingly stressful with each passing year too. Sometimes, I would work late into the night, or need to meet, from time to time, a client, or prospect with some of my other law partners.

Coming home after those meetings was tough for me. I knew what was heading my way and it usually did. I would enter the house, creep up the narrow staircase and there she was standing right in front of me. I knew she was upset. Her face said it all, taut as she stood there like a schoolteacher ready to hit me with a ruler, like the nuns did when I was a kid.

Then the stern tone of her voice and sharp delivery opened fire. "Where were you?"

In the tense silence that followed I shrugged, limply. "With a client…"

Then she said, moving in closer toward me, sniffing the air, "You smell like alcohol."

I started to get that hole in my stomach. I looked away, made a confused face, shrugged it off and admitted, "I had a drink, no big deal. I'm fine, okay."

And I was not fine. The white wolf was lurking. Then I increased her disturbed state of mind. "I'm going to have a drink *now*, I am fine." And I poured it.

On the questioning dragged. "Why do you need a drink?'

"I don't. I would like to relax for a minute. With dismay, I said, "Would you like something, a drink *perhaps*?"

"No," she stated fiercely.

I liked the fact the drink topic was getting to her. "Okay then, I would like *one* if that's okay," I calmly replied.

Then it got personal. And before I knew it: "Your family drinks too much."

I was exhausted. "Why do you say that? I just got home, it's been a long day and I just want to relax, have *one* drink."

"What did you do today?"

"Worked, I don't know." I thought, What the hell kind of question is that? I mean, what do you believe I possibly did today?

"On what? she retorted.

"What kind of question is that?" I asked.

Then the ordering started. "Read to the kids."

"I will, they are upstairs, probably watching something."

"You need to do their homework."

"I will. Let me just relax for a second, okay?

I did my best to bring her down a notch. I did not care any longer what she thought. Fights escalated and evenings out with clients and friends became more of a constant and I dreaded coming home after work and client meetings were my usual excuse for staying out. They were few and far between and I would meet up with friends or cruise certain restaurants and bars alone.

In New York, there is always some stranger there waiting to engage in conversation. I took advantage of being in the company of strangers since going home was not an option.

I could not, night after night, deal with the tension and fights. So, I waited it out. She would call me demanding to know where I was. And I would lie and say the meeting was running late.

~

Our marriage went on like this almost the entirety of 2004 and 2005. We spent Christmas in France in 2004. Collette made plans for us to spend New Year with her friend, Sandra, and her husband, in London where they lived. Leading up to Christmas, Collette was acting very strangely. She had recently started a part-time position at a modeling agency in New York. She started to dress like she was a teenager, wearing young clothes you would see on an eighteen-year-old. She used a lot of make-up which I had never seen before.

And she was very distant with me, and I became a stranger in her presence and I was disturbed by it all. And New Year's Eve arrived and we went to some contrived party where strangers booked tables and brought in the New Year together not knowing who each other was.

I remember staring at her from across the table that night, wondering to myself, *Why is that person hiding behind that costume?* Her black eye shadow blotting out her eyes, emaciated looking, dressed in teenage clothes and smoking one cigarette after another.

And I did not matter and I knew it. The next day, I was desperate to get out of London.

We stayed another night. That day Sandra and Collette went downtown to go shopping. I walked the streets of Chelsea with Sandra's husband, talking about life as we passed local pubs that reeked of cleaning fluid that covered the horrid stench of the puke that emanated from the streets in front of those British taverns.

I was a stranger to her. She was a stranger to me, so I thought.

~

In came 2005. She called me on February 4, 2005, while I was on a business trip in California. I was at a coffee shop around seven in the morning. She called me while I was waiting in line. She seemed nervous on the phone.

She started softly, "Hi, Maxwell? Where are you?"

I responded, "Getting coffee, why?"

She immediately retorted, "I think I might be pregnant…"

"How?" I quickly blurted out, staring at all the early morning patrons in disbelief.

I could tell right away she was a bit thrown off by my response. I asked how she was pregnant since we had not had sex for a long period of time.

She was silent for a second and said, "Well, I am not totally sure. I need to take a pregnancy test."

I responded, "I thought you were pregnant?" I continued to stare around the café wondering what was going on here. It made no sense.

In meek fashion she replied, "I think I am… I mean, I did not have my period. I feel it…" She then said to me, "If I am pregnant do you want to have the baby?"

I hesitated and without any thought tried to gather myself together since the whole thing was utterly confusing. The server kept asking me what I wanted. I finally woke up. "A large coffee, thanks."

I then returned to this bizarre call. "Absolutely. Yes. When will you really have a definitive answer?" It was a bombshell experience.

She stated that she needed to perform a pregnancy test and would let me know in an hour.

An hour passed. I was looking over Los Angeles by the pool at the Mondrian Hotel on Sunset Boulevard. My phone rang. It was her. "I'm pregnant."

My initial reaction to the news was that this was wonderful and might be the answer to getting our relationship on a better and happier path.

I left that hotel giddy, and boarded a plane for San Francisco, where I was to take depositions in a copyright case, I was involved in. The plane ride and the whole day were happy and joyful; I felt so peaceful and thankful, overflowing with gratitude.

I returned to New York with a sense of new beginnings. Perhaps things could change for the better. At first Collette seemed very happy, too, albeit for a brief period.

~

A few weeks after I returned home from California, she descended into uncontrollable crying and anguish that went on for several months; inexplicable bouts of sadness and tears flowed from her. I was worried.

Night after night, I would plead with her to tell me what was happening. "Collette, what is going on? You can tell me, please. This is crazy." She would refuse to tell me, night after night.

She then sought out medical help, but that did not seem to work either and she continued to devolve. I felt terrible for her.

For months, I saw her begin to surgically remove me from her life. I had felt like a stranger to her for many years now prior, but this was different, more certain. She was gone. I meant nothing to her, so I thought.

Her close friend, Luc, had just moved from Paris to New York. He became her right arm as she began spending most of her time with him.

Time passed, and Dori arrived on September 15, 2005. The birth was easy; she flew out like a perfectly shaped football into this world without a hitch.

~

My mother was very ill and insisted that Dori was not my biological child. I laughed and blew those comments off. During that period, my mother's disease, Scleroderma, (a hardening of her blood vessels that cut off all circulation to her extremities) was fierce, as it required that she undergo multiple amputations of her legs. I remember two months before my mother passed, she sat in her wheelchair and held up her left hand, her face emotionless and spoke. "Look, Max." I knew that extremity was the next to go.

She never complained and when I would come to her apartment, which was almost every evening she would peer up from her bed, her beautiful brown eyes, large and inviting, and say, "Oh dear, how are you. Tell me about your day?" She never wanted to focus on herself or draw attention to her horrible disease. Her mantra was, "As long as my mind is strong, I'm good with that."

.

~

I spent most of my time with all my kids, since Collette would usually say that she had already made plans with Luc. I accepted it, hoping the time spent with him would decrease her angst. He became a fixture in our home.

Arriving home from work and there was Luc at the kitchen table laughing and going on. He was short, razor thin, with a thick beard shadow and a tall clump of dark hair residing on his head.

He spoke in whispers. Luc would look up and give me a quick greeting. She would say, *Hello* and then return to her conversation with him. She was so excited when she was in his company.

I would sit at the kitchen table with them as they engaged in their own private conversation. I sat there, not understanding the rapid-fire conversations in French.

I remember one night when I arrived home I saw that he was eating a bowl of pasta. He would not stop talking that night, sputtering French in giddy frenetic, whispery tones. I watched as he was rapidly off-loading in French with a fork that stood still right in front of his mouth with a few strands of pasta on it.

He continued to rattle off in French with that fork dangling right up against his lips, remaining there for what seemed like an eternity. I wanted to take that fork and jam it down his throat. I fantasized about it sitting there.

Instead, I politely excused myself and went upstairs to bed.

I continued to stay away from home as much as possible. Like in 2004, I continued to make up client meetings to avoid coming home, staying out at night later and later.

I was looking for comfort. I continued to take refuge in the company of strangers. The marriage was crumbling. I just did not know what that meant or how we would end this failed union.

I could not come home, forced to wander New York. It was an awful feeling, and I was sad as I went from place to place in search of nothing other than a stranger to comfort me.

I would constantly think of the kids and let time pass. That was all I could do, so I thought. Our fights became increasingly worse. I was in pain.

~

That summer I went to France alone. Collette went before me, and we decided that I would go alone to see the kids. Her job presented a conflict so she told me that we would need to take separate vacation times.

So off I went. Prior to heading to the family summer home to spend time with the kids, I stayed for a few days in Paris at her grandmother's apartment. My time alone was wonderful.

Each morning I would start with a long run through the streets of Paris, traversing through tunnels, along the Seine River, watching the Parisians sunbathe on the banks of the river called Paris-Plage, and then up the Champs Elysées and everywhere else. It was amazing and a great way to experience the city.

I hit all the museums, like the Musée d'Orsay, that houses probably the greatest impressionistic art collection in the world, the Musée Picasso and several others.

I learned the Métro and would explore all of Paris. I spent a whole day at the world famous Sacre Coeur Cathedral and at night I would visit as many neighborhoods as I could find.

I learned so much about this great city and it was a blast. Collette never was that interested in this sort of exploration. I loved it. I could also see that my French was improving quite a bit. I would have dinner outside and just watch the people. I did not feel like a foreigner. It felt good.

I then took the train south to see the children which was quite relaxing and enjoyable. I left France with a smile.

~

Our last time as a married couple in France was the time we had Dori's baptism, which took place in December 2005.

We all left for Paris for the baptism. Collette was still in the throes of her 'ups and downs,' crying a lot and appearing very depressed. She had lost more weight than the year prior. I felt helpless. I could not comfort her. She would recoil every time I went near her.

Luc was by her side the whole time we were in France. We all prepared for the baptism. Her brother's friend, who had just been ordained as a priest, was chosen to perform the ceremony. He came by a few times to discuss the logistics of the ceremony, its importance, and spent a lot of time with us talking of philosophy, the Church, and other somewhat dense topics.

Collette was becoming increasingly angry with me. She went on about how I was not participating and was disinterested in the baptism, which was not true. She did her best to keep me away from it all.

I remember when we were driving into Paris to have dinner with her friend and husband, she was yelling at me about my purported lack of interest. I flew off the handle at her stating that it was she that was keeping me out of it all.

To get away and preserve my sanity, I ran every morning in the freezing December weather. I didn't care. I just ran to blow the steam off, sometimes ten miles and even longer. I found a forest that was perfect with large steep inclines that I would traverse and go on forever. It was my sanctuary.

Her mother also noticed Collette's erratic and emotional behavior. I remember pretending to be taking a nap next to the room where they were talking to see if I could learn anything, something that would give me a glimpse into her secret world and to what was happening.

It made no sense. I felt I was being kept in the dark about something larger but could not figure it out no matter how much I tried. I learned nothing since they would whisper and with my bad French, I could not understand what they were saying other than the periodic cries coming from Collette.

The baptism day arrived, and we all headed to the church. The ceremony went off without a hitch and we had a celebration gathering that evening. Luc was the chosen godfather, and he never left her side. I remember seeing them together after the church ceremony, she sitting on a chair while he, like a guard dog, was parked at her feet.

We stayed through Christmas and left prior to the New Year to go back to New York.

~

2006 arrived. Our final year together as a married couple.

That year was long and difficult, as Collette distanced herself from me entirely. The marriage was over. We were living separate lives. I did not even go to France that summer. It was pointless.

~

Prior to my departure in January 2007, I had a talk with her, openly and honestly, about something that had been bothering me for a long time; something I felt but could not confront her about.

It happened in late 2006. I asked her if we should seek marriage counseling prior to the divorce decision. I asked that question since it never came up before.

She bluntly said, "No."

I then asked, "Why?"

She quickly responded that it would be of no use. Her response gave me pause and led me to ask the ultimate question.

I asked her if she loved me.

She remained quiet for a few seconds, and responded, "No."

That response said it all to me. I needed to ask a further question, and that was, "Well, if that is the case, when did you fall out of love?"

She thought for a moment and said, "Years ago."

I did not say anything since there was nothing to say.

I did think to myself that maybe that was what I had been feeling for so long; that is why she acted the way she did for all these years.

That is the lack of love, I thought, *that made me recoil and act out*. In the aftermath of my *knowing* this truth the silence between us was final.

~

Looking back, I remember thinking of her bravery in those final moments. I mean there she was with three children and living in a foreign country, willing to walk away. Perhaps she sought acceptance that she never received the way she desired it. Perhaps she thought she did not belong. In truth, she was very young when she married me, left her family, and moved across the ocean to a country she was not familiar with. Maybe she felt lonely and knew I could not fill that void in her life.

~

I liked the place I had secured in January, but I was not prepared for this new and unexpected life: a life alone, without seeing my kids daily. Divorce is not fun, especially for the one, the man, who is forced to leave the family dwelling.

A lot of strange, unnatural things come over you: a shocking adjustment to the unknown, with random thoughts of trying to understand how this union dissolved so quickly.

My new apartment—the 'black box,' I aptly named it—was nice but empty. There were no kids to greet me at home after work, only dead, ugly silence.

Many things changed with the divorce that was an intimate part of my life. I left my home. I was alone in a strange new apartment. I no longer bathed my kids during the week, kissed or hugged them, had dinner with them, spent every holiday with them, watched movies with them, did homework with them, read to them, or played with them. I no longer took them to school. I was forced to adjust to visitation schedules. The weekends were too short. The departures on Sunday, or if we were lucky, Monday morning, to drop them off at school, were always stressful and sad. We all felt that way.

I could feel the tension building in the children as each hour passed, prior to their leaving on Sundays. The tension in us would grow with each passing hour. We would drag Sundays out as long as we could.

As the departure became imminent, the kids and I would get their bags together and take a taxi back to their mother's home. The ride was depressing and we all remained quiet, looking out at the New York streets as the taxi zigzagged through the Sunday traffic. We shifted in the backseat, all cramped together, bracing for the sharp turns.

Dori would begin to cry as we headed down the street and approached their home. On occasion, she would blurt out, "Why do we have to do this? I don't understand." I would do my best to calm her, hugging and kissing her, assuring her that all would be okay, planning out with her that we would do the next time we were together. She continued to cry. It broke my heart. I could not console her. I was helpless.

We had so much fun on those weekends. We spent a lot of time in the park, climbing the stone glacial striation outcroppings that can be seen throughout this oasis, rising above the surface of the grassy meadows. The children loved the park, running, going down the slides, and riding the swings and climbing the jungle gyms. In the spring and summer, my son enjoyed the Memorial Boathouse, where we would rent and navigate sailboats, watching them cruise in all directions across the small pond.

My daughters raced to the Alice in Wonderland bronze statue, adjacent to the boathouse. They were visibly mesmerized by the large, inviting fantasy figure of Lewis Carroll, creator of that iconic character, and they would climb all over it, sometimes all the way to the top, next to Alice's head, almost slipping sometimes, since the bronze icon had a slick surface.

We spent a lot of time at the Metropolitan Museum of Art, at the eastern edge of the park. The Egyptian exhibit was a favorite for us. We would explore this treasure trove of mummies, small artifacts, pottery bowls, figures, jewelry and symbols of that ancient time that were mostly glass-encased, with guards everywhere. We would do that for an hour or so before moving on to our second-favorite exhibit, the French Impressionist section of the museum. There the museum walls were adorned by some of the greatest Impressionist paintings in the world.

Dori would sometimes charge the paintings while I was busy studying the colorful masterpieces with my other two kids. She would come very close to these masterpieces; sometimes she would get too close, and I would see the security guard race over to her, to stop her small hands from touching the priceless treasures. I learned my lesson on those occasions, assuring the guards that she would always remain by my side to avoid any disasters.

Upon leaving the museum, we would visit all the merchants who lined up their makeshift tables outside the museum, mostly large card tables where the artisans would display their pieces of art and jewelry. Of great interest to my son was the display of handcrafted turtles that were beautiful and carefully crafted by various artisans, brightly colored, in all shapes and sizes, each turtle figurine with its own unique stone material. My son adored these displays and would ask me with much excitement to buy one or two of them for him. Naturally, we would leave with a treasure trove of new turtles that would augment his already substantial collection.

We would hit the stores, and upon returning home make dinners together on Saturday nights, cuddle up and watch animated movies together. We stayed up as late as possible, knowing it was our last night. Sunday would arrive, and the countdown to their departure would begin.

~

Alone, in my new place, the sounds of children anywhere outside of my dwelling would greet me with an extreme longing that would persist into an unrelenting pang, a longing that was painful, like nails being driven into my stomach. I constantly thought of my kids sixteen blocks away and what they must be doing. I learned to visualize their movements without seeing them.

The darkness that crept into my dwelling and mind at night was no friend. My nights, without my children, were difficult there, my sleep restless. I would toss and turn, waking up to then lie there during the night with thoughts racing through my head as I stared listlessly at the white ceiling. I thought of my youth, my parents, and years spent with my brother on the west side of the city that was so distant. I felt it was another life, never to be recaptured.

~

The first apartment Collette and I lived in as a newly married couple was down the street from the place I took that January day. It was a nicely appointed walkup where we set out to build our lives. We lived on the fourth floor. It was strange to pass by that apartment, a stark reminder of all that was ahead of us in our lives, now gone.

When I came upon our first home, I would stop and stare at the place, peering up at the fourth floor windows where we once resided.

Thoughts would ripple through my mind. *This was the place where we started out with so many dreams and aspirations; the place where my son was born.* I relived in my mind the moments we spent in that apartment as newlyweds. I would visualize it all, giving myself a mental tour of the place and happier moments that we shared for a brief time together.

Then I would continue down the street with a sense of loss. And one day I thought of my sister's wake. My parents wanted the wake to be at our house in the large room where my father had his study, next to the big fireplace. It was the room where the Christmas tree was always placed, the train circling around it during the holiday season.

As I entered the room, I saw family and friends everywhere. I remember looking to my left to see the coffin. It was brown, small and shiny. I could see part of my sister's frame in it. There were lots of flowers around the coffin.

I remember approaching the coffin, one foot in front of the other, and not wanting to see what I would have to confront. There was my sister, supine, her head resting on a pillow of white satin cloth, her body in complete stillness. She was adorned in a blue dress with a white collar. I stared at her figure and her face, a young, lifeless child.

I remember thinking as I knelt in front of her, how young she was to die. She would never get to go to high school, college, get married, raise kids, or experience anything. Never a chance to have all those things in life, *to feel cool*, so I thought.

I knelt and said some prayers and talked to her in silence. I stared at her again, trying to adjust my eyes, since her absolute stillness was unsettling. I then kissed her forehead and said goodbye.

I would often wonder peering up at that brownstone how I got here.

PART IV

CHILDHOOD

I grew up in a world run by men. My father controlled everything, down to the precise placement of an oriental rug that you were forbidden to step on. I remember always being forced to delicately step around that rug when going from one room to the next and it became a landmine.

Moving around the dwelling would be a problem too when my father was home from one of his extended business trips in Europe. He would abruptly and without notice close portions of the house.

"What are you doing in the living room?" he would say to me.

I would retort, a little surprised by the question, "Reading the newspaper, I guess…"

He would respond as if I should have known of the latest closure update. "Well, this room is closed and don't step on that oriental, I just organized it."

"Okay," and off I went, not really knowing if I was heading for another unexpected 'border' closing.

It did not help that he was an only child and a territorial man. He knew right away if you clipped a couple of dimes from his change dish that was strategically placed on top of his dresser. He pre-set the stereo sound to see when he returned from a trip if you fiddled with his music console.

My father required order but with so many kids chaos could not be silenced.

But not in his closet. There was no chaos on that army base. His expensive suits hung like creased military attire and his size fourteen shoes were positioned on the floor like black and brown battleships in a military harbor, impeccably aligned and shined. And his ties dangled like the flags of the United Nations in color-coordinated fashion from their own poles. And if you peered up, you'd be met with a collection of his business top hats, ordered on the highest shelf like soldiers saluting, hands cut and in an exact formation.

This was a major problem since I was a born slob. I thought I was kind of neat but not according to my pop, no. I remember when he would come back from his business trips all bets were off. I would pester my mom about his exact arrival. I knew what was coming and boy, it did. It was usually a Saturday afternoon when reentry would happen.

The black car would pull up to the front of the house and he would appear in his blue blazer, slowly lifting his tall frame from the back seat of the black shiny car, appearing very stiff since he was a stiff, most times wearing white or brown khaki pants, shoes shined, and into the house through the front door he would enter. Only my dad would come through that front door. Us kids would only be allowed to come through the back door and through the 'mud' room.

And up the stairs he went for a change of clothes and brief download with my mom and then back downstairs and into the sunroom he strolled with my mom for the big download on his trip. I was the server and poured the scotches and brought the Cracker Barrel cheese that he would voraciously consume as he told my mom that he had only eaten an apple on his long flight back from whatever foreign city.

A quick shake of his scotch glass and the sound of ice cubes colliding with a loud, "Maxwell, come in here, will you?" My signal to hustle up a refill. He would say as I entered, "Lad, a scotch, and get me another piece of that cheese, will you?

"Right away," I would respond dutifully.

Sundays were different. That was when I would wake up to the sound of the dreaded Bissel, that brown and gold hand push carpet dust cleaner that was his pal. I would lie in bed and hear the Bissell getting louder and louder, rolling over the carpet as it approached my room. I used to hope he would get distracted somehow but that was quixotic. The Bissell never failed to enter my room and my pop right behind it. "Maxwell, time to move, and what is the problem here? Your room is a mess. Listen, buddy, your mother is not a maid, you hear me?" I remained silent. I was trying to figure out what I did wrong and then, on one occasion I remember seeing out of the corner of my eye a piece of my white T-shirt hanging from the drawer of my dresser.

That little plastic duster he so loved and pushed around everywhere never cleaned a thing and my pop did not care about that. He was more interested in the lines it would create on the carpet. Sometimes, I would hear as I tiptoed about the house, "Maxwell, watch for the lines, I just vacuumed that room." I was trapped.

~

My dad was a highly successful businessman, a well-respected figure in the New York marketing and advertising community. He was creative and would lead some major marketing and advertising campaigns. He was a voracious reader, loved theatre and had a talent for drawing great sketches, on the fly. He was an excellent speaker and would mesmerize a room with his natural intelligence, business insight and sharp wit. I got a chance to see my father perform before an audience consisting of some top business leaders at the University of Pennsylvania. He held the audience effortlessly.

He was an honorable man and generous to the core. He was the guy who made sure everyone on my basketball team had new sneakers. He was a provider and worked around the clock to support his eight children. We were lucky as kids going to private schools and obtaining university degrees that my dad without hesitation paid for. We were blessed to live in a beautiful community and, unlike many of my friends, had a summer home on the beach.

~

In the 1960s, we would spend two weeks of the summer in Cape May, a bucolic community at the southern tip of New Jersey. This beach town was known for its beautiful Victorian architecture. There was a famous hotel, Congress Hall, where many presidents—including Abraham Lincoln—and other dignitaries would stay. Cape May is an old artistic community that offers a unique journey to the past.

We rented a small white house a few blocks from the boardwalk and the beach. There were lots of mosquitoes in Cape May, and most evenings a small truck, always at dusk, would spew into the soft, salty air plumes of carcinogenic gray smoke meant to kill those little biters. The kids would chase after that truck, absorbing the fumes on the way. There was Morrow's Nut House, the ultimate candy store, and Frank's Playland, where Skeet-Ball was the rage. Steger's was the one-stop shop for umbrellas, rafts, shuffles, buckets, and other toys.

I was told that Uncle Jack, who was elderly and whom I barely knew, often slipped off the beach in the middle of the day for a few libations. My brother Jesse wore his Philadelphia Phillies cap, his head always a bit tilted. Steger's also owned the blue huts that lined the beaches where small glass-bottled sodas and ice cream abounded. Those were the ultimate treats while listening to the Doors' number one hit that summer in 1968: "*Hello, I Love You,*" from their album *Waiting for the Sun.*

After years of those two-week frolics in Cape May, my parents bought a beachfront house in Avalon, New Jersey. It was done on a whim. My mother, as I understood it, convinced my father to make the purchase. Avalon was a small, undeveloped barrier island, thirteen miles north of Cape May. It was where we grew up during those wonderful summers as I reached puberty and became a young adult.

At the time, Avalon was an old fishing town. You would grab your breakfast at the local hardware store, where the restaurant seats were butted against the tool and fishing accessories section. The island was barely populated then. You could drive many blocks and not see a house. Only small homes would appear infrequently as you drove down its main corridor, Dune Drive, which stretched the length of the entire island.

I was told that a devastating hurricane had hit this small strip of beach sometime in the 1930s. It was an arid strip of sand, with little vegetation, but show cased gorgeous, wide-open beaches—virgin beaches that stretched that entire sandy runway. The hurricane recaptured two blocks or so, which now belonged to the ocean.

Avalon offered wonderful waves, especially in August. The surf was usually up since hurricane season had arrived. If the storm did not directly hit our soft, white, sandy strip—which was usually the case, thanks to North Carolina, which jutted out just enough to push those monsters back out to sea—the big surf would nonetheless roll to our shores.

I was younger than my compatriots and was usually the first one to witness these mountains of water breaking perfectly, with second and third breaks crashing far off the shores. You would immediately see their girth by virtue of the sprays, with a blowing west wind that would send the saltwater spray sky-high. A wild mist peeled away from these glorious titans. The beach break was another clear indication of what was rolling out there: huge, crushing waves that would require you to have exquisite precision and timing to pierce through the surf. You would paddle hard and get rolled as you were smothered in the saltiness of the Atlantic.

Part of the wonderment was the wide beaches, and a flickering ocean, all lit up. The waves brought massive ocean currents that would drag us along the shore with enormous strength, most times to the north.

When I was fourteen years old, I would paddle my surfboard out with my older brothers and the other surfing troops to capture these mountains of water. It took time to reach the largest waves, the last break far out in the ocean where the waves looked like tall buildings. Just when I thought I could judge the size of the surf, a surprise would greet me. I was scared and mesmerized by the sheer size of the wave, but that would not stop me from climbing onto that goliath for the ride of my life.

When the lifeguards came on duty at 9:30 a.m., we were called out of the water. That didn't stop us. We moved the party to designated surfing beaches, the two best being the Nuns' Beach and the 114th Street beach. The nuns, who resided in a beautiful beach front white convent, would migrate to the beach on those days just to watch us. By the end of the day, the wax we plied onto those surfboards left us with raw chests, and arms that could barely function.

How lucky we were to escape during those summers, unlike most kids, who were relegated to the humidity and overcrowded public pools in parts of northern New Jersey, including our village.

One thing is certain: when things were going well in my father's life he was happy; he was a proud man and the good things in life were important to him and he shared them with unbridled joy. Things changed when he was forced into retirement at the age of sixty. He did teach MBA school at a prominent university; however, my dad was built for the road and running in high business circles. That gave him his fuel, his energy and drive. Teaching was not enough for this man and it was at this time that manifestations of his depression appeared in his life.

~

And the late eighties arrived. And the abrupt sale of our homes and my father's disappearance to Europe, hiding from it all. And my memories from grade and high school like my work desk, books, sports awards, and photographs were simply lost, or discarded along the way.

It was at this time that our relationship got lost as my father's unhappiness grew. His humor left him, and reclusiveness and periods of frustration and anger took hold. I lost that sense of communication with him, and we fought a lot. He would view anything I would say positive about him as a father or his many business accomplishments as negative. In my mind, he could not see the positive in all he achieved, only his own perceived failures despite his great successes. My mom's illness at the time made it all that much harder.

I began to drift away from it all. I was locked out.

~

My mom laughed a lot, unlike my father who was serious most of the time, with flickers of humor that were intelligent, sharp. He worried a lot raising so many kids but my mom was a calming force and would say to him, "Oh, Patrick, just relax, everything will be fine." I remember my mom comforting him following his return home from overseas business trips.

Following those downloads from his European travels, I remember my mom once saying out of the side of her mouth to me, "I think his trip was more about sightseeing than work, or who knows what else." She wanted to be a lawyer but was instructed by her father, who was a successful lawyer and judge, that finishing school or a job as a secretary was it for her. She graduated from Trinity College in Washington D.C. with a mathematics degree.

~

And most men in my community were tough. The concept of cutting you a break if you fell out of line with the unmovable rules was not in their lexicon. You had to pay and learn not to do it again.

And there was abuse too. I remember him. He was a local lawyer. His head was huge, sitting on top of his tall frame. His large face looked like something out of a science fiction movie. He had oversized lips, a long head that looked like a half-moon, and a dangling chin that covered most of his neck. He had thick hands, clubby fingers, and a forward lean in his gait that invaded your private space.

His son, Tommy, was also large. He was a tough kid who dominated our conversations. He had a threatening quality about him, making you feel that you were forced to agree with everything he said. You never knew if he was going to hit you. He was a menacing figure who led the pack of kids, including me.

One time we were all in his living room, and Tommy was trying to start up the fireplace. His father, who appeared out of nowhere and was drunk, entered the room.

As I peered up from the floor, observing his massive presence, his look was chilling. I felt ill at ease as he stood there and leered at his son, not saying a word.

He finally muttered, "Tommy, what are you doing?"

"Just getting a fire going. It's cold, you know." Tommy's voice was cracking a bit. He was scared.

"Not enough heat for you and your friends?" His eyes appeared more menacing with each utterance.

"No, Dad, it's fine. I didn't mean that. I wanted to start a fire, that's all. We're just hanging out."

"Hanging out?" He turned silent again and stared at his kid. He slowly moved closer to the fireplace and picked up an iron poker and studied it.

I said nothing. I could see that Tommy was not the tough guy I was accustomed to. He was frightened, defending himself, almost like sending a plea to his father not to become angry or do something more violent. In that moment, Tommy's fear was palpable, something I had never witnessed before. It felt as if

Tommy was about to be beaten up by his father. I knew in that instant that this kid had been verbally and physically abused by this dad. It was obvious.

I, too, felt threatened by this looming figure. His eyes were dark, his silence deafening. I had no idea what this man was capable of. I felt vulnerable and wanted to run out of the room. Before I could think of what to do next, he kicked us all out of the house. It became clear to us that he was going to hurt Tommy once we left.

Not long after that incident, we all learned from Tommy that his father was abusive. Perhaps that was why he had to project his tough-guy image to us and others.

~

The women were a bit different although they hid from the men like us kids did, and it was survival of the fittest. As a young teen you never knew when you would be called upon to show your toughness. My problem was that I was not a tough kid and I was sensitive. My classmates saw this in me and took full advantage of it, except my friend, Malachy, of course. He was sensitive like me.

In junior high school I was constantly thinking about the last bell at the end of the school day and what awaited me outside. It was stressful, not knowing what to anticipate outside the school and whether I was going to get shoved around or thrown to the ground for a good after-school beating by the local thugs. I would head to the bathroom where the cool guys smoked for some intelligence gathering on what the after-school prognosis looked like for me.

Some days nothing would happen, just some stares guided in my direction, a light warning, and other days knives would be brandished my way. I was shoved, threatened, insulted and sometimes punched and kicked to the ground and that was usually the extent of these unwanted encounters. And I would dust myself off and move along, back home.

My looks did not help me either. I mean I was a tall gangly Irish kid, twelve or so years old, with a face full of pimples and braces that could light up a town. The tough guys were mostly Italian kids with solid facial hair, well-built and cool clothes like shiny black leather jackets and tight blue jeans, gold chains hanging from their necks.

~

The homes in my town, mostly Tudor style houses, were freakishly enormous. They housed large families that made up my community, some with nine kids, and others with twelve or sixteen. I never thought I came from an extremely large family, given what I witnessed around me—just the norm, as I had seven siblings. This raucous Irish community butted against Newark, New

Jersey, only thirty minutes by train from New York City.

This town doused most times in the drink, edgy and lost, hosted many of the men who returned from World War II. And they had come home from the war decades earlier in search of new meaning against the losses and atrocities they confronted daily on those battlefields, the mental and physical wounds still fresh in their minds, even with many years passing. These veterans didn't talk about the war. They were silent. They moved on with life.

My mother's brother, Uncle Phil, was no exception. My mother told me that he came back from the war a changed man. It was not until his early eighties that he would speak of his experiences.

A strong man that never flinched, he had seen it all. He was a war hero; a fearless marine captain fighting in the South Pacific, Okinawa to be precise, against the Japanese who were, by all accounts, ruthless and unrelenting.

My cousin Michelle, his eldest daughter and the family matriarch shared with me her memories along with newspaper articles that reported on her father's heroism that earned him the Silver Star and Purple Heart metals of honor.

According to the reports, the USS Clay was sailing in the Pacific to an unknown destination. Many of the marines that were on board, including my uncle, thought they might be heading to mainland Japan; instead, these marines landed on the beaches of Okinawa where some of the bloodiest battles of World War II took place.

I learned that on April 16, 1945, Uncle Phil, the commanding marine officer of "I Company" led the charge of his military unit that successfully sealed seven heavily fortified caves atop Green Ridge, crushed the largest enemy military pocket obstructing the Japanese drive up to Motobu Peninsula, a highly strategic enemy position that allowed the Japanese to control the entire west bank of Okinawa Island.

My uncle returned after that decisive victory with a volunteer rescue squad to save one of his wounded men, and successfully evacuated that soldier in the face of heavy machine gun fire. For the Silver Star award citing my uncle's bravery and valor, his commendation read, *"His daring, fearless leadership, indomitable fighting spirit and devotion to duty were an inspiration to all the men in his company and in keeping with the highest traditions of the U.S. Naval Service."*

Later, my uncle led his company to Sugarloaf Hill but was wounded near Shuri Castle, an area that was not far from Sugarloaf Hill, on May 14, 1945. He was transported Stateside on the USS Solace. He was awarded the Purple Heart. I learned that it would be more than fifteen days of ferocious fighting before the marines were victorious in one of the bloodiest battles of the war.

~

The women of this community also remained silent. They raised large families, and for the most part constructed their lives around the men they married. I witnessed tension and dysfunction among the adults. They were restless souls. I often wondered whether the large families they had given birth to offered them a sense of importance, or whether they were the product of their cultural longings, their heritage. The women feebly attempted to manage these war veterans' losses and pain, sometimes becoming collateral damage along the way.

This constant struggle led to many fights that often resulted in broken marriages. The community was in a slow state of decay. In many of my friends' homes, it was natural for me to see separate bedrooms for their parents. The children, mostly unkempt, aimlessly wandered the neighborhoods at night—wild, lost kids looking for trouble, stealing booze from their parents' liquor stashes, having no curfew, and avoiding the dysfunction that awaited them at home.

~

This hamlet, however, was scenic, beautiful, almost magical. As a child, I soaked up those streets that swept throughout the village, lined perfectly with huge oak trees, gas lamps at every crevice of the rolling, undulating avenues, where you would find a multitude of kids playing everywhere. The main street was adorned on both sides by little shops where everyone knew you, and you knew everyone.

~

I made my daily commute to elementary school, Our Lady of Lourdes, the family parish where the community would gather on Sundays. I always took a shortcut that required me to descend a steep incline and cross a brook behind the biggest house of all. I felt that stone, dark-brown home was haunted, with its spiraling roofs in different shapes and sizes covering that massive structure. I would pick up my pace, heart racing as I cut through that scary place to get to the brook. The brook served as a meeting place where my friends and I would hang out sometimes. And if we were lucky, we would get some guy to buy us a few six packs of beer and it was special to us, our private hideaway.

My friend Malachy was sometimes there. He would never participate in the banter that my other friends were engaged in. He had no desire to talk about girls, clothes, booze, or anything that was of no interest to him. Malachy kept a distance from everyone. When we left those gatherings, he became more alive with me; he was released from a forced encounter and was now free. I was like a student of his, trying to grasp as much as I could.

I knew Malachy since my early childhood. We were neighbors. He lived not far away; a stone's throw up the street from my house. His small, gray home was tucked far back from the street, intentionally hidden from public view. The house did not look at all like the other homes in my community, paint chips peeling off the sides, a place covered in thick, tangled vines that enveloped the structure like a gigantic spider web. The lawn was overgrown, with patches of dead grass scattered across the front yard, totally unkempt. It was spooky looking, like it was possessed by some supernatural being.

I felt that he did not want me to come into his house. I never said anything about it. I was too uncomfortable to ask why. I thought he might be embarrassed or was hiding something. I did manage to come into his house occasionally.

Prior to entering, I felt a change in him. He became distracted, nervous. I could feel his demeanor was off as soon as we entered, like I suddenly morphed into a stranger to him.

At the front door, he would never look either way, and would rush me feverishly through the first floor to the entrance of the basement from the kitchen. That was where we would spend all our time, either playing pool on an old, ripped, dull green pool table, or listening to music.

Malachy had two identical Alaskan huskies who would roam through the house. They were beautiful dogs that would appear out of nowhere from time to time. They never barked but would, from a slight distance, just peer up at me. I thought it unnatural that Malachy would never address the dogs or pet them. It was like he didn't even see them. When I would ask Malachy about them, he would give me a quizzical look. It was as if they were not even there to Malachy, like ghosts wandering the dwelling. I could see their breath since the house was so cold.

It was awkward to be with Malachy. We were close, yet there was this subtle distance between us that he desired. I felt he had so much to say but could not let it out. I never knew what he was thinking. We were best friends with an unknown between us, something I believe we both knew was there but never talked about.

He was secretive, a loner, like me. I was his only friend. We hung out a lot; he never would mention other boys or girls that he socialized with. My other friends never talked about him.

~

Malachy was tall and his hair was always tousled. It was long and covered his eyes. He intended it that way. Malachy was hiding behind something. We connected only so far as he would allow. Our conversations were mostly topical, rather than deep exchanges about life.

His eyes, piercing blue, served as my guide to where he was floating at any given time. They would take a slight turn to the north when he began to lift off into his own world. He had beautiful eyes, but you could never tell him that. He never liked any form of admiration directed his way; it was repugnant to him; he would recoil for a moment and then regain his balance, slowly. He rarely changed his clothes but was always clean. He liked plaid shirts and blue jeans. His clothes did not fit him, they hung off his thin frame. He couldn't care less.

He loved movies. That was our biggest connection when we were kids and young adults. We grew up in the seventies, so we got a front row seat to the best of the best. Filmmaking at that time took off, with new actors who set an entirely disruptive course in the genre, like DeNiro, Pacino and so many others. These guys were great to watch, always with this psychotic bent, a loner quality they put out there effortlessly. *Taxi Driver* was a favorite of ours to see together.

Malachy never said this to me, but I felt him wanting to be that guy on the screen. He could not do it in real life, or so I thought. Sometimes I would study him while watching one of those movies and see a different person; he was engrossed in the film. I often caught him mimicking the actors' lines. He was at peace in those movie-watching moments.

He was very intelligent. He never tried in school but performed well. He was wise beyond his years. I would catch it in an observation, or a phrase he would utter from time to time that would conjure a deeper thought in me, like he saw something that most people would not see. It was amazing to experience.

Malachy was a voracious reader. He loved nineteenth-century Russian authors like Fyodor Dostoevsky. On the way home from the brook one afternoon, he wanted to talk about *The Brothers Karamazov*. He was interested in the chapter, 'The Grand Inquisitor,' which explored, in poetic prose, ideas about human nature and freedom, and its fundamental ambiguity.

"There are many messages in Dostoevsky's writing," Malachy said as we walked. "Those guys you hang out with would never understand."

"How do you know that? I've never talked about literature with them."

"They aren't smart enough to understand someone like Dostoevsky."

"Copy that, Malachy," I said. He was starting to make me angry with his condescending tone.

This didn't stop him. "He takes you to deep levels, you see. He forces you to think existential stuff."

"Okay."

"You understand what I'm saying?"

"Kind of, Malachy."

That didn't satisfy him. "Well, what I'm saying is that he was very prophetic, you know. He used lots of metaphors and dense prose that only a few people back then could understand. You know why?"

"No." I shrugged.

"He was protecting himself from confronting repercussions from an oppressive Russian regime. His writing would, unbeknownst to them, attack their way of life, their corruption and dominance over the people. The rich and empowered wouldn't tolerate anything that could possibly be construed as an attack on them. In my mind, he was a true existentialist. He was so engrossed in it all."

I had to admit that he'd gotten more out of reading *The Brothers Karamazov* than I had. I wasn't really all that interested in his opinions, but I thought the best way to deal with Malachy was to appear engaged. We were still several blocks from home. If he didn't think I was paying attention, he would keep hounding me. "I don't think I understand all that as well as you do," I said.

He bit the bait. "You should read it again. Just go slow. It's very dense. If you read it too fast, you'll miss his messages."

"Okay, sure. I'll read it again, I promise. Then we can talk about it some more."

"All right." He seemed pleased.

I just shrugged and kept walking.

"I got to go," he said. "See you later."

"Okay, Malachy, see you soon."

In a blink, he was gone. Malachy was like that. When he decided it was time to go, he just seemed to vanish. I was glad to see him go. A little Malachy went a long way.

~

This bucolic village where I lived was in a deep valley, and approaching it required a steep, almost vertical descent from the mountain that stood to the south. While my town was mostly Irish Catholic, a thriving Jewish community had a foothold along the slopes of the mountain. Many of my dearest friends were Jewish, and most came from successful and accomplished families. They maintained a more considered and relaxed approach to life than their Irish counterparts in the valley.

At the center of this deep valley, a magical train cut right through the village. The Erie Lackawanna train was a rusty, old, brown, passenger train that still had foreboding black shades from the war. The train made a pleasant humming sound as it moved slowly from the station, always precise in its arrivals and departures. The seats were covered in a worn-out cloth that gave off a musty smell. It served as the main source of transportation for all the inhabitants of northern New Jersey. This train was like a moving repository of history that captured and stored the events of the lives of those it carried, etched indelibly into its fabric and girth.

And like clockwork, my father and the multitudes of other young men would hustle to catch that bit of history in the early morning hours, their brown and black hats perfectly positioned, dressed like the movie stars of the golden era of the 1940s. They boarded this moving treasure, wearing camel hair and wool overcoats in the winter, seersucker or linen suits in the summer, always with a work bag and newspaper in hand. They spoke to one another in low tones as they walked the platform and climbed the steep, steel staircase onto this trusted friend, heading to their respective places of work.

This was where the fun for us began. My friend Johnny—sometimes other guys too, but mostly Johnny—and I would descend on that platform for some entertainment. We were young, maybe ten or eleven years old.

Johnny was funny as hell. He was a chubby, round-faced kid with a long, pointed nose that held a tint of red. He was a scoundrel. He was always in trouble or looking for some. He couldn't care less. The guy was trying to cop beer when he was eleven years old. He would steal his parents' cigarettes and light up when we would meet at the train station. He was constantly laughing, making fun of the men boarding the train. "Hey, look at that poor working stiff. He climbs that train like he's going to his death. It must be the job, poor idiot, or maybe his wife. Right, Max? She probably whacked him upside the head on the way out the door—make money or don't come home."

I tried to keep him focused. "Johnny, you have the coins?"

"No, I thought you brought them." He then pulled on this cigarette and released the smoke towards the sky.

"What!" I said in disbelief.

He then lowered his eyes staring right into mine, hesitated with a slight impish grin and said, "Just messing with you, Max boy... or Maxwella, should I say? Just kidding."

I ignored him. "Here she comes. I can hear that humming sound."

Then the train hummed into view. Johnny was out of the gate, scrambling ahead of me. He moved with determination down the steps of the cracked and decaying concrete crossing overhead, landing that round, pudgy frame of his on the train platform, and jumping with a butt hanging out of his mouth onto the thick stones that rested next to the steel, shiny tracks. I wasn't far behind.

As the old train bore down on us, the tracks began to vibrate and gave off a smoldering smell of steel and electricity, palpable to all the human senses. We feverishly placed our pennies on the rails and jumped back as the train glided past us. We waited for the last car to pass, then collected those coins, the face of Lincoln flattened beyond recognition.

"Look at this shit!" Johnny screamed, his lower belly now protruding from his shirt as his hand stretched to the sky. "Lincoln got shot!"

Unbeknownst to my parents, we would ride that train without a boarding ticket, just to experience its glory. We closely observed the morning commuters. I thought they were fun to watch as they jockeyed in a frenzied effort to secure their places on the musty seats. Once they found their desired spots, they would quietly read their newspapers, with no audible conversation, embroiled in the news of the day, periodically observing the towns they passed along the way.

Johnny nudged my shoulder and pointed at two guys. "Look at those stiffs. They're like robots with those old movie star hats."

We moved from car to car to avoid the conductor, since we had no money. We didn't want to be excused from this private, joyous adventure. Johnny would let out loud, howling screams as we exited from one car to the next.

I tried to shut him up. "Johnny, what the hell are you doing? You're going to get us caught."

He kept going. "Don't worry, these guys are half-asleep. A little wake-up call. No big deal."

The rides back home at the end of the day were vastly different. The men boarded the train after a few libations, octaves at full tilt, laughter, arguments, loud conversations that touched on all topics, hats tilted and ties pulled from their necks. The newspapers were strewn about the cars, plumes of cigar and cigarette smoke abounding. These men came home disheveled, as their day was over. They disembarked the train, navigating those steep, narrow steel steps, spilling themselves onto the platform and lumbering on back to their homes.

This was where it sometimes got ugly, especially if Johnny was in the mood for a drink and started looking around for a loose beer. He could see some of these men were half-baked, so that was his opportunity to lift a few tall boys.

"Hey, that guy over there. He's dead asleep. See him over there? Yeah, aisle seat. Good. His hat is covering half his face. He's out for the count, and he's got three beers. See them? Yeah, unopened beers, cold ones, in that six-pack. Let's get it."

I wanted no part of this. "Johnny, no! We're going to get nailed. What if one of these passengers sees us? We're dead."

Johnny came right back. "Time it, Max. Timing is everything. You know I've done this caper before, and successfully I might say. Have some faith, my man. When the train starts to get close to the station, we bolt. First, we calmly grab the beer, eyes straight ahead. Don't make any eye contact, okay? Head right to the middle exit and hop off. Easy stuff."

I knew there was nothing I could say to change his mind. When Johnny had his mind set on something, forget about it. Go along or get out of his way.

Johnny quickly moved down the aisle, his eyes looking straight ahead as I followed behind. The men on each side didn't notice us. They were embroiled in conversation or passed out.

Johnny approached the drunken commuter, who was snoring lightly. He quickly looked behind to make sure I was right behind him. He gingerly bent down a little, and with his left hand, slowly picked up the plastic tie holding the remaining beers and moved quickly to the exit platform. He kept his head positioned straight ahead with a slight lift above the crowd. I must say, he was quite deft at this little caper.

As the train moved into the next station and slowed, he jumped off. I followed him and leaped off right behind him.

Johnny plopped down on the ground in a thick wooded area out of the departing passengers' sight. I watched as he cracked a beer and fired up one of his parents' smokes. He took a big gulp, looked up at me, and gleefully exclaimed, his beer held high in the air, "Max, victory! I told you it was no big deal." He took another swig at the can, now pointing his right chubby finger right at my head and in a professorial deliberative manner. "Max, the *obvious* is the *unobvious*, right?"

"What?" I was confused by the bit of philosophy Johnny was aiming at my head. Johnny maintained a full library of one-liners designed to confuse the listener that he would use on me and others from time to time.

It was his way of making a point or justifying something that he knew deep down was wrong.

"Nobody on that train was even thinking about what we were up to, and yet it was *obvious*, but to them not so *obvious*."

I agreed, letting that new bit of the Johnny philosophy go. I envied his fearless tactics. Johnny got used to the fact that I wasn't going to indulge. He was fun to watch though. Johnny was more interested in stealing beer off these men than riding the trains.

~

Johnny was always on the hunt for booze. He would make me come and hang by the local liquor store as he quietly solicited random folks to buy him beer. I would stand off to the side where no streetlights were present, hiding there in the dark where I wouldn't be noticed.

Johnny would place himself proudly right in front of the store and pace back and forth, adjusting his ill-fitting pants that were always stained and stretched out of proportion to his rotund lower half, frequently peering through the two large glass windows. He had a clear view into this small liquor store and did his best not to get noticed by the owner, who would from time to time step out of the store to patrol the surroundings near his place.

The street wasn't far from the big Catholic university, so there was a good amount of foot traffic.

Many drunks would pass by this store, fumbling along, uttering inaudible sentences to each other, or just hissing or mumbling to themselves. The area was a bit seedy and the streetlights dim.

Johnny was laser focused. He was going to get that six-pack, and that was it. He just needed that one guy to cop beer for him. Johnny carried a couple of crinkled-up one-dollar bills in one pocket and a heavy amount of change in the other pocket: quarters, nickels, and dimes. He would peer about, a cigarette hanging out of his mouth, patiently waiting for that one person he thought might be game. The longer the hair and the more hippie the look, the better the target for Johnny.

When the first hippie-like figure would approach the entrance, Johnny would say, almost in a whisper, "Hey, mister, can I ask you a question?"

Upon hearing Johnny's light, whispery voice, the guy would stop, appear slightly confused, and look around to see this kid standing there in a shadow, hands in his pocket, rattling his change. "What do you want, kid?"

Johnny was polite and generous to the stranger. "Can you cop us a six-pack of beer, mister?"

"You're a kid," the man typically replied. "What are you doing?"

Johnny was prepared for this response since he had heard it many times in the past. "I only want to get a six-pack. That's all, mister. And you can have a beer for helping me."

Most passersby's would say, "Get lost," and keep moving on.

Johnny was resilient and had no problem with rejection. It fueled his mission. As he said to me countless times, "Max, it's a numbers game, the law of averages."

I would nod in agreement, hoping he wouldn't get busted.

Then the perfect target would arrive. Perfect targets were those that appeared a little drunk themselves. Johnny would convince the passerby to cop the beer, sometimes being forced to give up two beers, but it worked. Johnny got the beer and slipped out of sight and onto a quiet side street, where he would plop down curbside, his butt crack on display, and drink the four beers that were left.

~

Johnny suffered a tragic blow of his own when he lost his only brother, Chris. He fell through a glass bubble on top of a building at Tufts University. His friend was on top of that glass bubble and fell through. They were watching the solar eclipse. Chris tried to save him. He dove through the bubble to his death. His friend survived.

Johnny's family changed when his brother was taken away so unexpectedly. The day he died, I came by his house and saw state troopers parked in front of his home. The blinds at his house were drawn. I knocked on the back door. Johnny's mom opened the door, and said I needed to go. She was upset. I left. I knew something horrible had happened.

Following Chris' death, I would come by the house and see Johnny's father, a former World War II Navy man, chain-smoke Camel cigarettes at the white Formica kitchen table and drink coffee. He died the day his son died.

He was a slight man with a heavy Boston accent. His face was gray. He read the newspaper without uttering a word, drank his coffee, and smoked his cigarettes. He was curt with me.

Johnny told me his father had a fight with Chris before he went back to school. That was their last exchange. It was a turbulent time, with generations clashing over lifestyles. Chris smoked pot. He had long hair. His father disliked that. They fought; a younger generation and older folks of a different era that could not see eye to eye.

Chris's room was on the third floor of that house. It was an attic he had turned into his bedroom. It was painted green and cluttered with posters of musicians that adorned the walls; a stereo set with large speakers was the fulcrum of his room. We spent a lot of time in his room. We would listen to all of Chris's music and talk about life and, from time to time, his brother. Chris's music was a great distraction. I loved to listen to Bob Dylan. Johnny did not. He did not like his voice. I insisted that Dylan was about lyrics and that he was a great poet. Johnny did not care. He liked The Who. I liked the Rolling Stones. Johnny was good with that.

Johnny was stoic and did not show a lot of emotion during the times we spent in his brother's room. The music was his comfort. He chose the albums his brother liked best. Those were the ones we played.

There were those rare moments in the attic when Johnny would talk of his brother. He was trying to process his brother's horrific and unexpected departure. "Max it is strange, you know."

I would ask, "Why?"

He would lean back and slowly fall to the floor, staring up at the slanted ceiling and say, "I don't know, things are strange now. I keep asking myself why him, why not me?"

I knew he was feeling guilty that it was his brother who died and not him. He was grappling with how all this turned out. "Max, you know, one day he is here and then bang, gone, just like that, in a second."

I did not know how to respond. I tried to make him feel better though. "Johnny, that is out of your control, you know it."

He responded quietly, "Well, it didn't have to be. I mean, why him and not me?"

I had no answer. "I don't know, Johnny, life works in crazy ways. It can be arbitrary. I get what you are saying, but you have no control over this. It's awful. But that is how it turned out, you know? Sometimes, things just happen for no good reason."

I could tell that he was absorbed in his own thoughts. This was not the jolly Johnny I was accustomed to. Then he said, lying there on his brother's bedroom floor, still gazing up at the ceiling, "Well, I guess you're right, but I got to tell you, my pop, he is so different now with me. I feel, and I could be wrong, that when he sees me he can only think of Chris, of what he lost. I am an ugly reminder."

I had no words. I asked, "Why do you feel like that?"

He thought for a moment, and said, "He is bothered by me. He treats me differently. It feels as if he wishes it was me and not Chris."

I had no idea how to respond to that. But I tried as best I could. "Johnny, your pop is trying to process this horrible thing too. Maybe he is suffering and can't express himself right now. You know, like pulling back on everything."

"You think?" Johnny observed. He continued, "I feel when I am in his presence, he recoils, he has nothing to say. It's strange but I feel that I remind him of what he lost and he can't handle that, you know?"

I thought for a second and tried to be comforting, knowing that my efforts probably would not amount to much. I knew that Johnny, despite his stoicism, was in a lot of pain and certainly confused as to where he stood with Chris' passing. "Johnny, your pop loves you, he just needs time and a lot of it, like your mom, to process this. It's normal for any parent, you know. He loves you but right now can't express it. He is somewhere else."

Johnny sighed. "Yeah, makes sense I guess. It's just this feeling, you know. I mean, I feel like I have no idea how do deal with this, like I'm just floating... somewhere, you see?"

"I get you and it is normal. You, like your dad and mom, are grieving. This was a tragedy and no one expected it."

He sat back up and spoke to the wall, not making any eye contact with me. "Well, Max, I guess that's the way life rolls. I miss him so much."

"I get that Johnny and so do I."

Johnny then became silent and we both continued to listen to his brother's records. There was nothing else I could offer. I could only be there and comfort him. That was it. He was just a kid and this was life changing for him.

~

His mother took residence in the kitchen when her husband was not there. I do not recall them being in the same room after Chris' death. She was such a nice person, always insisting we eat something. She was short and plump and had an inviting smile. She had the gift of gab. She spoke to us all the time as she smoked her Parliament 100 cigarettes.

She positioned herself against that white refrigerator as she spoke to us, lighting one cigarette after another. She was in pain and could not process her loss.

I came by a lot during that period. We would eat something and then move to the other room and watch *The Honeymooners*. We laughed. It was an escape. I thought of the man in the kitchen sitting at the white Formica kitchen table. He had checked out.

~

Growing up Irish Catholic came with a good dose of religion. Like some of the other homes in this community, my house was inundated with religious artifacts that appeared at every corner in our large Tudor-style dwelling that sat angled on a downward-sloping street. The hallway, living room, and bedroom walls were saturated with religious portraits of saints, martyrs, and other religious icons that were there to greet you.

A portrait of Christ in the Garden of Gethsemane, where He prayed the night of his betrayal and arrest, was prominently displayed as you ascended to the second floor. The house had six kids' bedrooms. In each bedroom loomed a large cross above the bed, with a patron saint next to the crucifix. A plastic bottle of Lourdes holy water stood on the night table. A plethora of religious figurines rested, perfectly content and straight up, on tables throughout this sprawling home, peering straight at you as you sat on a sofa or a chair.

My parents' bedroom made me think of a Catholic priest's room. There were two single beds, one for my mother and the other for my father. Large crucifixes peered down at both beds, perfectly aligned, and a Bible rested on the nightstand. On the walls of the room were religious paintings. I knew that was my father's influence, since my mother was a discreet person when it came to religion. She never pushed religious dogma on you. My father did, to control everything.

My father, Patrick Thomas —or 'Patrick' as he was always referred to—was a staunch Catholic. Religion empowered him with a sense of importance, offering answers to what he couldn't reconcile.

To make matters more interesting, prior to meeting my mother, he was a seminarian, and I was told that he became an ordained Catholic priest for a brief period. I remember seeing a picture of him in his vesture when he was about twenty-four years old. Tall, dark, and handsome, with piercing blue eyes that jumped from the photograph, he stood proudly in his religious robe, white collar pressed against his neck, almost choking him.

I was told that my father left the vocation shortly after the end of World War II. Thereafter, he met my mother, and following a brief stint stateside in an army camp somewhere in Louisiana during the Korean War, he married her. My mother told me he taught the soldiers how to use firearms. She said that he was not a happy soldier on that base. He disliked the locker room noise that emanated from the soldiers, and he found the heat of those Southern nights intolerable in the summer. He wanted out of this forced military duty.

My father collected numerous paintings on his business trips to Europe. Pictures of strange towns, of Old-World city scenes, and of bucolic countryside landscapes hung on many walls in the house. Smoke a cigarette or cigar, and you would find that the ashtray you were flicking your ash into was from some fancy hotel where my father had stayed. He loved those hotel ashtrays. For him, they were a remembrance, a reminder of where he belonged.

He was an only child, now raising eight children. This came with many obligations, mundane at times. I remember how awkward he seemed to me sometimes, and I felt bad for him. My father required his space, and Europe offered him that escape. The older he got, the longer those business trips became, sometimes lasting three straight weeks at a time. His periodic reentries home began to feel like momentary visits before he departed again to another place in Europe and other parts of the world.

I once got a view of his world when my younger sister, Tammy, and I accompanied him on one of his trips to Europe. One evening, we were coming back to the hotel from a dinner with Hans, a business colleague of his. He was a thin man, almost transparent, and short;

a handsome man who dressed impeccably. He was visibly lit that evening and sat perched forward in the back of the car, next to my sister, while my father drove.

I sat in the passenger seat. Hans was constantly leaning forward, settled between two front seats like an annoying three-year-old, speaking fast and loud, exposing in graphic detail the nights my father and he would spend indulging in drink and chatting up women. He blithely offered up one story after another. There was no stopping this Danish man.

As the stories unfolded, I saw that my father was increasingly agitated and furious.

"Hans, stop it and shut up," he finally said. "What are you talking about? You've had too much to drink. Now just sit back and say nothing."

Unfortunately for my father, his reaction only fueled Hans to keep the stories coming.

Hans was visibly pleased, laughing and frothing, exposing with delight all the frolicsome details on those nights. "Patrick," he said with a heavy Danish accent, "come on, you remember. We were crazy that night."

I listened intently. My father surreptitiously glanced at me to get a read on my reaction to these tales. I gave him no clue as to what I thought about the veracity of what this little Danish man was spewing from the backseat of the car. I was interested in the stories, and watched my father hold that steering wheel tighter and tighter, his face constricting so much that he looked almost disfigured.

Once Hans was ejected from the backseat of the car at his hotel, my father began to mitigate the damage. It was clear to me that Hans was telling the truth, despite anything my father offered us to defrock the man. I got to know a part of my dad that night, and it felt good.

My father was an interesting character. This I know. He was eccentric, he loved fashion, he loved to shop and buy the best for himself. He was the guy who would arrive at the party with an ascot around his neck. At the same time, he was the pious man, the one who disdained, in his words, materialistic people. Yet he was in awe of the men who were successful in life. He craved their presence. He tried to emulate them.

~

My mother encouraged him to see more of his local community, and he would agree, although I knew he had no interest in that. It was a forced obligation to him. The neighborhood parties were a theater of the absurd, as my father did his best to impose the Old World onto this local group that, aside from serving in the war, didn't care about Europe, or really about any other part of the world.

The local Irish in this community were insurance salesmen, construction workers, coaches, policemen, teachers, lawyers, and doctors, all quite content with their immediate surroundings, never thinking about or desiring anything outside their protected microcosm.

This was where the infrequent parties that my parents would throw went sideways, my father being the trigger. I was the designated server, so I had a front-row seat to the comedy of errors that would unfold.

At the start of one such gathering, my father passed by me with a pithy acknowledgement. "How are you doing, lad?"

Before I could respond, he was already on his way down the winding staircase to greet the partygoers. He wore an ascot tightly wrapped around his neck, and a blue blazer on his large frame. The shine on his shoes almost blinded you. I remember the French music faintly emanating up to the second floor from the large, wooden RCA console.

When the party began at our home, most of the guests were already on shaky ground, since their party had started prior to their arrival. Wobbly figures of all shapes and sizes entered the house, then gravitated to the makeshift bar in the kitchen, poured themselves drinks, lit cigarettes, and began to engage in local gossip. I saw my father observe the crowd first and then engage in conversation with various guests. I could tell he was uncomfortable as he approached them.

He had a few humorous openers, his icebreakers that never resonated with the group. "So," he would utter, "how are things here?" Before anyone in the group could respond, he would continue. "I'm exhausted. Geez, I had a long trip that took me through most of Europe. You know what time it is by my body?"

The group seemed totally confused, offering no real response, just nodding politely, acknowledging his utterances without any understanding of where he was going with this.

My father continued. "Say, have you read the book *Mary Queen of Scots*? Very interesting. I read it on the plane from Paris."

It was obvious they were totally lost. It was pure comedy. Then at some point, he would release a line in French on a passerby, who would look at him quizzically and keep moving. I could also tell that the crowd was trying to figure out the costume he was wearing but said nothing. The ascot around his neck was the draw.

Mr. Clarke, a local insurance salesman, lived up the street with his wife, Anita. He was a regular at these gatherings. They had nine kids. The middle child, Tim, was my friend. He was a good-looking kid and a great athlete. Mr Clarke was a stocky, short guy with a booming voice and huge bald head. That head of his was a beaming beacon of red, veins protruding out of his forehead when he would blast anything out of his mouth. He loved to drink. The more he drank, the louder he would become and the redder his head would get. He thought my father was a snob.

One night Mr Clarke stumbled over, his whiskey glass half-empty, tilted in his hand, and cornered my dad. His face leering up at my father, he fumbled with his words. "Hey, Patrick, how's the madcap tours through Europe going?" He was mocking my dad in an attacking fashion.

My father didn't get it, I thought. He blithely responded, "Oh, John, I got to tell you, I had a chance to meet the French president at a dinner. You know him—François Mitterrand. Very intelligent man."

My father's response fueled this drunken reveler.

"Who," he blurted back, bits of spit flying out of his mouth. "I hate the French! Those little bastards. They still think they won the war. I was there putting my ass on the line for those little baguettes. I mean, my God, Patrick."

My father let the response roll right off his shoulders. He enjoyed his putative dominance over this man. "Well, I must say, they have their economy right."

I was in earshot of this exchange and quietly listened. It was sport for my dad, and each salvo coming from my dad only agitated this man more. He shot back, "What! They're socialists... commies." Before my dad could respond to that, Mr. Clarke said, "Patrick, have a drink."

"John, that's a go. How about you?"

"That would be great there, Patrick."

I came in from the side and asked my dad if I could pour the drinks.

This time my dad said, "No, lad, I'll do it. See if anyone else needs another."

They both made their way to the makeshift bar in the kitchen, Mr. Clarke stumbling a bit as my father led him, walking in front of this poor drunk with a hidden agenda.

I knew what my father was up to, since I had witnessed this before. My pop wanted to pour that drink, and a lot of it, into Mr. Clarke's glass. My dad was wearing him out, the drink being the weapon of choice. The drunker Mr. Clarke got, the better for my dad, since in his mind, the gathering would end that much sooner.

He would engage in this mission with other partygoers. I knew that each time he would take over the bartending duties.

On this occasion, I followed my father and Mr. Clarke into the kitchen. Pretending to be cleaning up some of the mess, I tossed a few empty beer cans into the trash.

As they headed to the bar, Mr. Clarke was carefully negotiating each step, one foot in front of the other. "Hey, Patrick," he said, "Patty boy, you, my man. You got to be chasing a few skirts. Yeah, yeah, come on, world traveler."

My pop didn't acknowledge his statement. He was on a mission. He grabbed that bottle of whiskey and dumped the liquid into Mr. Clarke's glass and then shoved an ice cube or two in with it. Mr. Clarke was blind to everything around him and saw nothing other than this big glass of whiskey coming his way. He stared at it, and without saying a word, gulped down half of it.

My pop never poured himself a drink. He was stone cold sober and intended to remain that way. He was in control. He then returned to what he was saying.

"John, got a lot of work. Plane rides are long, you know."

Mr. Clarke could barely keep himself from falling flat on his face onto the oriental rug. Finished with the Europe thing, he was looking for another angle. With some resignation in his voice, he abruptly changed the subject. "Yeah, not really, Pat," he mumbled. "Anyway, your son, Max, has got to get it together on the court."

"He seems to be doing fine, don't you think?"

"How would you know? You're never there to see him."

My father defused him immediately. "Well, he does have some talent, but he needs a better feel for the court." He left it at that. "Cheers, John."

"Right back at you, Pat. The ascot is working."

"What?"

"Your ascot, Patrick. Is that a French thing or what?"

"No, not really."

"Geez, thanks, Patrick. You make a nice pour. Talk in a bit."

"Great, John, great."

Mr. Clarke was not one of my favorite people. He would often come to our Catholic Youth Organization basketball games. He was lit up every time, his head always bright red, peering out from the stands. I could see those trademark protruding head veins from the court.

The heckling would begin from this man. He shouted, "Dylan, *what* town are we in? Come on."

I tried to ignore him. Tim did too.

But he wouldn't stop, and his voice would get louder with each utterance. "Dylan, come on. Where are you? Play defense! Come on, get in the game." He would shriek, "Get in the game, boy! *Defense!* Get your head in the game! For crying out loud, where are you? Come on, Dylan, think."

Well, it goes without saying that I couldn't think on the court with that bald, drunk loudmouth screaming at me from the stands. He was obnoxious. My coach would tell me to ignore him, but it was tough, since the basketball gym was small. That man's voice engulfed the whole place.

I could see that most parents knew he was hammered. His wife, Anita, would sit there by his side and pretend nothing was going on. She was drunk too.

~

As the party at our house dragged on, things devolved. The locals were agitated by my father's behavior. The booze flowed with alacrity. I made my last round among the partygoers to see if anyone wanted a refill, a last call. My pop put me up to this since he was now ready to end this forced obligation. He was tired and bored.

I made my final tour and could see that most of the crowd was done. I looked over at the sofa near the fireplace and caught a glimpse of Johnny's father struggling, like he was slowly being sucked into quicksand. He always claimed that end part of the sofa at these events and never moved off it. There he was, a short, thin Navy man, his head bobbing up, down, and sideways as he tried to lean himself into the side of the sofa to avoid falling face forward down onto the brown coffee table.

His voice was loud as hell, speaking into the smoky air, as no one was talking to him. There he was, alone, having a conversation with himself. I could see he was finished. His hair was askew, his shirt now out of his black pants, and the ashtray in front of him full of spent, smoldering cigarette butts, a few of them resting on the floor. He looked sad to me. I watched him lean back to retrieve a pack of cigarettes from the front pocket of his stained white shirt. He managed to lift one out of the pack and stuck it in his mouth. I saw that he couldn't find a light, as his hands were feeling up his pockets in search of one.

I quickly moved in to light his cigarette. He was bleary-eyed as he slowly looked up from the sofa. He leaned forward and pushed his neck up so I could fire it up.

When I would go to Johnny's house, his father never really acknowledged me. He'd say, "Hey," and then go back to his paper. He smoked his unfiltered

Camel cigarettes, head down and absorbed in the paper at the kitchen table.

That wasn't the case at these events. He was a totally different man, drunk but highly engaging, throwing his hands out toward me, waving them in my face to make me sit down with him. I told him I had to keep working and asked him if he needed anything to drink. He didn't respond. He was done. He wanted to talk, that I could tell, so I stood there waiting to see what was on his mind. I bent over toward him since it was noisy in the room, and his voice was barely audible. His breath reeked of cigarettes and booze.

He tried to be engaged. "Maxwell," he said with a thick Boston accent, "you like that school you're attending?"

Right away, I knew he just needed some company, since his question was a bit perfunctory. I was okay with that. I felt bad for him. Johnny told me his father and older brother, Chris, were constantly fighting prior to the tragedy.

"Yes," I responded. "Things are fine."

"Well, I thought you'd be better off at the school where Johnny goes," he retorted, slurring his words. "Well-rounded kids, you know, and a hell of a curriculum." His finger pointed straight up at the ceiling. He was a professor and didn't much care for sports, so he kept the conversation focused on academics. He was never without his plastic pencil holder peering out of his top pocket.

"Yeah, Johnny's school is great," I said. "He likes it a lot. It's something to consider, what you said."

He liked that. "I think you're approaching it correctly." Pointing his finger up at me like a professor, he leaned forward and muttered, "Education is all you got at the end."

I agreed. I could see his eyes were beginning to shut. I asked him again if he would like something, but he didn't respond. His head slowly slumped, and he passed out. I left his side.

As I turned around, there she was, Mr. Clarke's wife, Anita, sitting on a straight-backed chair holding court with her girlfriends. She was something to watch: a tall, comely woman with bleach-blond hair that stood high and bright red lipstick lighting up her thin lips. She wore a floral dress. Her skinny brown legs were crossed, she was showing them off in her high heels.

She dangled a long cigarette delicately from her hand, and her long, painted nails in bright red matched, I thought, her glossy red lipstick. She summoned me over to her chair.

Here we go, I thought. "Hi, Mrs. Clarke. Would you like something?"

"Yes, in a second. How are you?"

"I'm fine, and you?"

"Oh, Maxwell, you look so handsome tonight." She fluttered her hands at me. "I haven't seen you come by our home lately. Timothy is doing so well. He's my star, like you, my dear." She looked at her friends gathered around her, expecting them to agree, and they dutifully did. She ran the show. She was the gang leader. She had a strong personality. With a husband like Mr. Clarke, I thought, she had no choice. That man had a temper.

Timothy was the middle child, like me, and unlike the rest of her brood, he was a talented, handsome kid. She worshipped him.

When I would come by the Clarke house, Mrs. Clarke was often stretched out on a lounge chair off the kitchen out on her deck, her tiny bathing suit glued to her emaciated frame, sunbathing. Oil glistening from her entire aging body, she was in her moment, oblivious to the hordes of kids running around the backyard, some of the older ones taking refuge in the garage, drinking and smoking reefer. She was only concerned with keeping her tan up.

In the late afternoon, it was common to see her and her friends' playing cards in the living room. They would play cards all afternoon while they drank their Highballs or Manhattans. She ran the game, shouting across the room to her son, Kevin, "Kevin, fix the drinks!"

Kevin was gay. He loved to play piano and was good at it. I liked him a lot. I knew old man Clarke disdained him. Kevin was tall, with a thick frame, but when he opened his mouth, he had this light, soft voice that was in complete contrast to his massive figure.

Mr. Clarke knew his son was gay, but he would never, at least when I was there, acknowledge him. It was like he wasn't there or was a misfit prop. When they had their parties, which went on to all hours of the evening, toward the end of the night, Mr. Clarke would sometimes go to the bottom of the narrow staircase and yell, "Kevin, get down here!"

Kevin would reluctantly appear. It was obvious that he had seen this before.

"Come on, play that thing." Mr. Clarke said, pointing fiercely at it. "That piano, boy. Go play it." Then he would turn to the guests. "See. He can do this, at least."

Kevin would play that thing. I would see Mr. Clarke making faces at his guests as Kevin played. I thought this was a circus act for him. His guests, or at least some of them, looked uneasy. I wanted to hit him right smack on his bald red head.

I felt awful for Kevin and could see that he was crying.

Anita was afraid of her husband. When Mr. Clarke would arrive home, her card game ended right then, and the women scattered like termites that were hit with a blinding Klug light. I saw the fear in her face.

He was a tough guy and could get physical with his kids, depending, of course, on his mood and the amount of booze he swallowed prior to his arrival. Timothy's older brother, John, double-bolted his bedroom door. Mr. and Mrs. Clarke slept in separate bedrooms.

I again asked Mrs. Clarke if she would like something to drink.

She thought for a second, looked at her posse, and giggled. "Yes, dear, just one more. You know, the usual."

I thanked her, and off I went to the kitchen to pack her a stiff Manhattan. She was expecting nothing less. As I entered the kitchen, I heard the phone ring. I picked it up. It was Johnny and he seemed very rushed. He was slurring his words. I knew with his parents at my house he was well into their liquor stash.

"Hey, Max, Johnny here."

"What's up?"

"Is my pop still there?" he muttered incoherently.

"Yeah."

"Good. Is he polluted?"

"Yeah... I mean, I think so. Why?"

"Where's your old man?"

"In the other room."

"Good, keep him there."

"What?" I exclaimed. I knew what he was planning.

"Where's my old lady?" His voice became more and more demanding.

"I don't know," I responded. "Somewhere." This was the last thing I wanted, I thought. *Why did I pick up that phone?*

He shot back, "We're on our way."

"For what? Why?"

He laughed. "Booze, my man," he quickly stated. "Booze, Max."

I knew right then that he had planned this all out, and I could tell he had already been nipping heavily into his parents' stash but didn't want to get caught drinking all their booze. I pleaded with him. "Johnny, come on, man, not tonight, please."

Johnny retorted with complete confidence, enunciating each word slowly, "Just leave the back door open."

"Johnny, please, come on. I don't want to get caught."

"Caught!" he shouted. "Come on, Max, your old man won't know the difference. He's oblivious, and you're sober and the waiter. I got this. Trust me. If he sees that supplies are a bit low, just say you served them up to the crowd."

"Served what?" I asked, totally frustrated with him.

"I don't know, Max," he said calmly. "The beer or something. Is there some hard stuff still there?"

"Yeah," I replied, wishing I had said that we were cleaned out of the hard stuff. Johnny would not have believed me anyway. He knew we had a healthy booze cabinet since he would secretly grab a bottle of something on occasion and stuff it in his coat, or down his pants.

"We'll be there in a few minutes."

"Johnny, really?"

"Don't worry. I got this."

Before I could respond, he hung up.

So now, I had to keep going to the kitchen, checking to see who was there prior to Johnny's arrival with his gang. I also had to do recon in the party room to make sure no one came into the kitchen. I kept circling around with everyone, asking if they wanted another drink, since I wanted to keep them away from the kitchen. Most important was my pop. He was sober and pacing all over the place.

Then, as I entered the kitchen, I heard some muffled laughter outside, and the back door flung open.

There was Johnny, crazed and all lit up. "Max, the guys are right outside. Let's move!"

I watched as Johnny looted the place. The guy had brought a pillowcase with him. He grabbed a bottle of vodka, and then flung open the refrigerator door. As he bent over and stuck his head into the refrigerator, his butt crack was there to see. He swept the beer into the pillowcase. Then he raced, the bulging sack thrust over his shoulder, out of the back door and disappeared into the night with a quick smile back at me. "Thanks, Max."

I could see a few of the other guys laughing. *What an opportunist*, I thought.

Johnny did cross the line many times. Once we went to a local fancy Chinese restaurant, the only one in our village. It was late, and Johnny was drunk. He grabbed a menu and ordered all kinds of Chinese food.

"Johnny, what are you doing?" I spoke. "We don't have any money."

"So what?" he replied.

I wanted to leave, but Johnny wouldn't have it.

"Don't worry, Max, it's all good."

"What's good? We can't pay for this stuff."

"I got it."

"Got what?" I exclaimed.

"Just watch."

When the waiter left, Johnny got up and raced toward the bar. He was aware that the bartender was in the kitchen, and this was his opportunity. He climbed over the bar and grabbed a bottle of booze and hopped back over.

"Come on, Max, let's get out of here!"

Well, the bartender suddenly appeared and started shouting that he was calling the police. Johnny never looked back and scrambled right out of the joint, laughing all the way.

I was shocked. *We're dead*, I thought.

Johnny darted across the street, bottle in hand, and ran toward the brook where we would all gather. He sat, cracked the bottle, and took a big swig.

He grinned at me. "Max, you need to relax. We didn't get caught, right?"

I had no words. I just sat there as Johnny did his best downing the bottle. Before we parted, Johnny took a last huge hit off the bottle and hid it in the bushes.

"Max, we got tomorrow's stash," he muttered my way. He laughed to himself and started to head home. "Max, you got to relax, man. It worked. See you tomorrow."

This guy is out of control, I thought to myself. One day, he's going to pay for his nutty behavior.

~

The night was getting late, and I was tired. I saw out of the corner of my eye my pop talking to the mysterious Mrs. Keene. This woman was the best-looking lady at the party, and she never took off her huge, round black sunglasses. She reminded me of Mrs. Robinson, the mother in the film *The Graduate*.

She was the one person that my pop liked to talk to. She carried herself in a regal sort of way. She would lean against the wall and peer at the crowd. She looked bored. She never engaged anyone in conversation, other than my pop. She held her cigarette in a long black holder and would periodically draw off it and tilt her head up as she let the plume of smoke slowly spill from the side of her mouth toward the ceiling.

Her husband never came to these parties. I often wondered if they were still married. She acted like she was on the move and my dad was the target. She was waiting for the moment. I could see her following him with her eyes as if he were the only man in the room.

Well, my dad liked her too. She would indulge him when he talked of his travels, taking a keen interest in his business and business trips, asking all kinds of questions while maintaining a good command of politics, various cultures, and the world. He loved that.

When he would say something, I would hear her high-pitched laugh, like she got exactly what he was saying and could absolutely identify with everything he would espouse. "Oh, Patrick, I couldn't agree more," was a constant refrain of hers.

I would gravitate their way and listen to their talks. It was hilarious. I thought she was messing with him. I thought at least my pop had one in the crowd that he could connect with.

When I would catch them together, I would blaze their way and ask, "Mrs. Keene, can I refresh your drink?"

Before she could respond, my father would answer for her. "Lad, yes, get her another." He would turn to her and follow up. "You *are* having a scotch, right? With a twist of lemon?"

I could tell she loved that he knew her drink.

"Oh, Patrick, you have one heck of a steel-trap memory. I love your ascot. Where did you buy it?"

He loved it. "London," he said.

"Oh," she responded, "I love that city. It's so interesting,"

I could tell she had never seen the place. My dad didn't care. He was delighted to have an audience. It also gave him an opportunity to go on and on about all his travels.

I mean, my father was a foreigner to these townsfolk, except, of course, Mrs. Keene. So, the crowd, like most people do, judged him and got more pissed with each confrontation they had with him. I thought it was funny since my dad couldn't have cared less. In fact, I thought he enjoyed the attacks and judgments. It made him feel superior to these people.

As the evening rolled on, the conversations became louder, more heated, the sidebars among the locals more frequent, my father floating around, oblivious to it all. He was content knowing the end was near.

My mother tried to placate everyone she could talk to. She was totally engaged in their conversations, always asking questions, offering herself up to the townsfolk, trying feebly to divert their attention from the elephant in the room—my father.

The invitees were now visibly hammered and had had enough, it was apparent. The crowd dispersed soon after, some almost falling out of their chairs, others mumbling incoherently as they made their way to the front door.

One lady had a freakishly large frame. Her face was enormous and possessed manly features. Her hair was erect and stood high as a tall ceiling, jet-black hair doused in some off-the-shelf hair dye, immobile. I saw her moving toward the front door and descending the outside stairs in front of the house, grabbing the railing to avoid a spill. She was drunk. Those stairs were steep, and I feared she might plunge down them. But she managed to reach the bottom without falling flat on her large face.

With her back to me and my father, she did an about-face, angled herself, and leered at him. She pointed her finger at him and shouted in a drunken tone, "Patrick, you are a snob!" Then she sent another salvo. "Who do you think you are?" She managed to turn and start stumbling toward her car. My father didn't appear at all disturbed by her verbal assault. He was happy the party was over.

~

And there was unrest in my town and around the country. Newark was on fire, with the military positioned everywhere, some less than a few miles from where I lived. The crux of this violence was the Black community's response to untenable living standards and discrimination they confronted daily.

I watched nightly telecasts of the Vietnam War. This was the first conflict that was televised, and I saw the carnage that was ongoing in Southeast Asia. This was coupled with telecasts of demonstrations and riots across America, including in New York City.

I attended a basketball camp at the university. At the edge of the campus, there was a house painted in a vast array of bright colors and usually quiet. A community of Black students lived there. I believe for the most part, they were students at the college.

The Black Panthers, a radical black group founded in Oakland, California, wore black berets and military outfits. They came through that dwelling. I saw them from time to time. They would come and go while I was attending a summer basketball camp at the college.

One morning we were all outside doing layup practice. The basketball courts faced this mysterious house, and out of nowhere a young Black man came charging out of the house toward us, screaming, while rapidly stabbing himself in the chest until he dropped to the ground, dead. We were all sent home that day and the July heat was daunting.

I remained quiet that day. My friends didn't talk about it. I could not get that young man out of my mind. He was in so much pain.

The turmoil and unrest throughout the nation also made its way into many homes with kids and parents. The World War II generation and the hippie generation were at odds. There were constant fights about long hair, pot, and unchaperoned trips with girlfriends. Everything was out of sync with these competing generations. I just watched it and played a lot of basketball in the backyard to avoid arguing, especially between my brother, Jake, and my father. I didn't make any judgments as to who was right or wrong. I had no real basis from which to opine. It was a clash of generations with vastly different lifestyles.

I did pay a lot of attention to the war. I don't know why, but this ongoing televised event captured my interest. I had an opinion about it, although given my youth, I might as well have been talking to myself. My friends were totally disinterested, since their focus was on copping beer and finding women.

The Vietnam War was in full throttle. Johnson was at the helm, and then Nixon. Johnson decided not to run for president for a second term due to the turmoil the war was causing: division; riots; a new and outspoken generation, rebellious by every standard; demonstrations; the Kent State University massacre, under Nixon's watch and order. Soldiers fought an invisible enemy, the North Vietcong. The Vietnam War continued to rage and Nixon presided over the conflict. I never disliked Nixon, even during the Watergate hearings. He lied, but so did every other president. He just taped himself.

The nation was confused. It was losing the sense of infallibility that infused the country following the success of World War II. We were fighting on impossible terrain—as in Afghanistan and Iraq today—against an invisible enemy: a woman, a child, a man dressed in civilian clothes.

The body count was fifty-nine thousand killed. It left a nation in chaos. There was no warm reception for the young men who made it back, no parades for these soldiers. In fact, disembarking a plane fresh from the battlefield, they were spit at, yelled at, and called 'baby-killers.' I felt an overwhelming sadness and empathy for these forgotten soldiers.

Cocaine and LSD became the thing. The promoter of the popular drug LSD was none other than Harvard professor Timothy Leary, with his famous, (or infamous) phrase: 'Tune in, turn on, drop out.'

My neighbor Kevin had long hair and was a Vietnam vet who loved to play basketball in my backyard. I was thirteen or fourteen. I thought he was disturbed—probably with PTSD, or shell shock, as it was called at that time.

He was a nice guy. He trembled. He had a listless stare, like nothing was behind those eyes of his. He also walked a little funny, with a slight angle to his gait. He would come by and play basketball with me a lot. He was quiet. We never had a conversation. He wasn't ready for or interested in any form of communication. I respected that. We communicated through the game, which he enjoyed.

Then there was the infamous My Lai Massacre, the murder of unarmed South Vietnamese civilians in the Son Tinh District of South Vietnam, which happened on March 16, 1968. That incident was highly televised and talked about. It was a horrible event. Between 347 and 504 unarmed civilians were massacred by US Army soldiers from Company C, 11th Brigade, 23rd Division. The victims included men, women, children, and infants. Some of the women were gang-raped, their bodies mutilated.

While twenty-six soldiers were charged with criminal offenses, it was only Lieutenant William Calley Jr., a platoon leader in C Company, who was convicted. He was originally given a life sentence, but it was reduced to three and a half years. I recall that he was on the cover of *Time* magazine. I read the article.

I was really disgusted by this lost cause. I thought of Kevin, my basketball buddy. What did he experience and see in Vietnam?

Things changed after that atrocity, which prompted global outrage when it became public knowledge in November 1969. The war was essentially over, as the massacre fueled domestic opposition to US involvement in Vietnam. The public rebuked any further involvement in this chaotic, lost cause. The nation was exhausted.

I was surprised, though, that the Vietnam War persisted despite the massacre. President Nixon continued his pursuit, including the Cambodian invasion in 1970 that substantially widened antiwar protests at home and angered many members of Congress, who accused Nixon of having broadened the war illegally. There were many hearings on that subject. The rest is history. It took five more years and a communist takeover of South Vietnam for American forces to fully depart.

The fall of Saigon—that was something to watch on television. Saigon was captured by the People's Army of Vietnam (PAVN)—also known as the Vietcong—on April 30, 1975. This event marked the end of the Vietnam War and the start of a transition period to the formal reunification of Vietnam into the Socialist Republic of Vietnam.

We hustled out of there. I watched the televised footage of Saigon as hundreds feverishly clung to tilting, gray choppers.

~

Johnny and I lost touch after high school. A few years later, though, I was walking down the avenue to catch a train to New York City. I had a job interview in the city to be a paralegal. As I was moving toward the station, I glanced across the main street and saw an overweight figure with a blue cap and a large black duffel bag making his way up the avenue.

I recognized that walk of his, that lumbering walk, his head down a bit and the butt hanging out of his mouth. At first, I just stood there on the other side of the street and watched him. I wasn't sure whether it was a good idea to disturb him. I mean, we had lost touch several years prior, and he pretty much didn't want to continue our friendship at that time. But I thought of all the great times too, and the things we went through together, the loss of his brother Chris, and my sister Mary. We were kindred spirits despite the distance that ensued between us. I went for it.

I jogged across the street, dodging cars, and continued to watch him. I knew it was now or never. It was strange for me to think that we had been so close, yet on this day, I felt such uneasiness about reconnecting with him. "Johnny, it's me," I yelled. "What's happening?"

He stopped and turned toward me as I was running at him from the street. He dropped his duffel bag. "Max, oh my God. What's going on, man? It's been forever."

I could see that he was truly happy to see me after several years of no contact at all. I asked him how he was doing.

"Man, I'm in Boston now, finishing college," he responded. "Yeah, can you believe it? I'm almost done with the whole thing. What about you, Max? What are you doing?"

I explained that I was in my last year of college too and heading to New York to try to get a summer job.

We exchanged a few lines, general in nature, about our lives, and then the conversation sort of went flat. An awkward silence took over.

Johnny said a few parting words. "Well. Max, what a surprise. It's good to see you."

I responded with the same.

That was the last time I saw Johnny.

~

As I walked on to take the train, I thought of how supportive Johnny was when we got the news about my sister. We met under the orchard trees in a grassy meadow at the top of a hill from where I lived. I remember it was a beautiful spring day.

Johnny was instructive and soothing, beyond his years. After a few minutes of silence sitting under that orchard tree Johnny looked up at the blue sky and asked, "So, Max, how are you doing?"

I nodded. "Okay, I guess… My mom is pretty upset though."

He thought for a moment and then calmly observed, "Well, Max, sometimes things happen… I don't know, but they do, you know? It's hard, I know that…"

I listened. I was mute, thinking about my mother at the kitchen table. I felt so bad for her. I hated to see her suffer like that. Then I thought about my sister. "She is so young, she's a baby, how come her?"

Johnny stood up and walked a few feet away and looked out over the orchard trees. He grabbed a pack of cigarettes out of his pocket and fired one up. His back was toward me as I saw him take a long drag off his cigarette and exhale it, delivering a large plume of smoke toward the sky.

He then turned my way and as he approached me, our eyes met. "Max, I know it's tough. I question a lot of shit, you know. I sometimes just question it all. Everything is so arbitrary, you know. I wish I could do something; you know. I get your pain. I just can't make it go away for you. I guess now you got to be strong for your mom and your sister… She's so young, a baby. She has no clue. But you got to be strong for your mom and dad. They got to deal with this craziness."

I listened and without saying a word nodded in agreement. I thought he was right, but I felt numb. I also knew he was thinking of his own loss. Johnny then asked, "Max, with the cancer, did they say how bad it is?"

I didn't have an answer but said, "Well, they want her to get to the hospital right away for all those treatments, like now. So, I can only imagine that can't be good, right?"

Johnny sighed, thought for a moment and pulled on his smoke. "Yeah, that's probably not a good sign," he said, smoke pouring from his mouth. He then followed with, "Max, remember, you never know, she is a baby, maybe they got ways, you know?"

I knew he was doing his best to make this horrible news less awful, but it was what it was. "Johnny," I said, "it's so weird that kids, babies get sick like this. I mean, they are so young. I don't get it."

I remember time was getting late. I was starting to feel anxious. I thanked him. I knew I should go back to the house to see how my parents were doing. Johnny understood. He leaned into me and gave me a hug and parted down the street toward his house.

I walked slowly home in thought.

~

On May 22, 2003, my brother Jake and I found my father dead. He was at a rehabilitation facility recovering from an illness that struck his heart. When we arrived at the facility, the miasma greeted us immediately. The place was cold and depressing.

I knew something was wrong. The orderly and nurses were crying. They passed us off to a doctor, who advised us that our father had died only a few minutes earlier. He escorted us into a room where my father lay dead in a small bed. I saw that he had been paddled to save his life. He was a tall man, and now in death, he was a shrunken corpse, almost unrecognizable. I was forced to adjust my vision just to get a sense of who he was. It was disturbing to see him like that.

Jake kept touching my father. I did not. I just stared at his shoes. Shoes can really tell a story. I continued to stare at those shoes that rested next to his bed, size fourteen, staring right back. I saw his life through them. So many random emotions hit me as I stared at his shoes. It was as if a movie reel of his life passed through my mind. I asked myself, *Is this what it all comes down to at the end of a life?*

I wanted to let him know what could have been, if only he could have seen the wonder of his own existence later in life his and his considerable   personal and professional accomplishments despite life's hardships and setbacks. I wanted to let him know how much we all loved him. I wanted to have a dialogue with him that never happened.

I felt he willed his own departure. He did the math and decided it was time to go. My father had no reason to press on. The fight had left him. Depression can exact this on some people.

My childhood years flew through me. This person that I stood with made my wonderful childhood possible. Sadly, he didn't allow himself credit for all the good he bestowed on me and others. He loved my mother. I wished he could have loved himself in the same fashion. His life would have been more joyful.

I don't blame him for leaving this way. I do, however, carry a sadness that continues till this day for all the possibilities that could have been his to enjoy in his golden years. It never happened to him, and that is the sad part of his life story.

I will say this: as adults, we carry our childhoods with us wherever we go. I never saw him clearly. I long to go back in time to see the man he was with wiser eyes.

~

My mother came down to say goodbye to her husband. At the time, she was hospitalized at Columbia Presbyterian Hospital. She was in bad shape. My sisters, Maggie, and Kate got her out of Columbia Hospital and came down to the scene.

From her wheelchair, my mother touched my dad's neck, bruised from all the pounding of the paddles, and bade him farewell. She cried silently and spoke to him in tones that were barely audible. She touched his bruised frame, so delicately, with soft strokes of her hand against the side of his bruised head and neck. She leaned forward in the black wheelchair and stretched her hands onto his lifeless body in a loving way, like she was soothing a restless, crying baby. She was engaged in a conversation with him. It was her goodbye to a husband of nearly forty years. She loved him.

Both of my parents are gone. My mother died in July 2009. She was a mere fraction of herself after several amputations and died of heart failure like my father. Two angels married in 1953 with aspirations, dreams, and goals. Now departed.

PART V

THE MOST DECEPTIVE OF TIMES

October 24, 2007 was a brisk and beautiful fall day. My mom died that July. I headed to Central Park for a run. The park was crowded with runners that Sunday since the New York marathon was only two weeks away. I planned on a short run. It turned into a twelve mile trek through the park.

I circled the park and I was overwhelmed by random reflections that would come and go about Dori and the events leading up to her birth that I ignored. Mother's illness and the protracted divorce blinded me.

My run ended. I then walked for three hours around various areas of the park. I thought about that phone call I received in California from Collette in the early hours of the morning: *I might be pregnant but I need to take a pregnancy test to make sure*. That conversation made no sense.

I mean, one would take the test prior to concluding, "I might be pregnant." Her voice on that call was off, in hindsight. I thought, *She was shaky, nervous sounding, hesitant in her speech. She was feeling me out.*

The math did not work. If, as she stated, she was pregnant, when could that possibly have happened? That would have been January 11, 2005, the last time we had intercourse. Prior to that time, nothing for almost a year. Then, I thought about our other two children. It took us months with precise timing to get her pregnant and now one encounter led to a pregnancy. Highly unlikely, I thought.

The test confirmed her pregnancy on February 4, 2005. That math meant that Dori would have been born seven and half months into her pregnancy. She would be a premature baby. The day Collette gave birth no doctor mentioned this, which would be mandatory.

Then I moved to the entire pregnancy itself. Why was she so depressed and crying all the time? Why was I surgically removed from her life and the doctor appointments leading up to the birth? My mother's insistence that the child was not mine... I wrote it off at the time due to her illness, however she was lucid and very forceful about the whole thing. Collette's desperation to escape and get back to France.

These unplanned reflections swirled in my head. I called my sister, Maggie, to ask if I could stop by. I told her we needed to talk.

"Yes, come over, now."

As I walked to her place, I knew what to expect. Her voice said it all on the phone. This issue had been raised by her and others many times prior. I ignored it.

~

I arrived at her apartment. She opened the door quickly. "Come on in," she said briskly. She rushed me into her kitchen as I followed her. She lived in one of those old, white-glove, beautiful apartment buildings on Park Avenue where the lobby was a throwback to a 1940s' film and the doormen were mostly Irish.

Her pre-war apartment had high ceilings with beautiful moldings that extended throughout the spacious dwelling. There was a huge, oversized living room that you would see as you exited the foyer and peered down a short, wide entrance way. The living room was gorgeous with a large fireplace, wood crafted in precise detail.

The layout of her place was designed for the earlier inhabitants as a second home for dinner parties, a getaway to the city from their country homes, like most pre-war apartments that lined this iconic avenue.

The dining room was also large with wood paneling that wrapped itself around the room. There was a huge master bedroom and a small area off the kitchen that once was where the help would sleep, now converted into her daughter's bedroom. The floors were solid, old wood with patterns exquisitely designed and always shimmering.

The apartment maintained a warmth and captured throughout the day slivers of light that would land on the expensive oriental rug that rested in the expansive living room, a black Steinway piano in the corner that was covered with beautifully framed pictures of family and friends. Beautiful furniture with intricate linen and silk patterns perfectly positioned for conversation and social events.

She opened a bottle of red wine and lit up a cigarette, talking rapidly as she blew the small puffs of the cigarette out of the side of her mouth up the loud steel hood fan, which hovered above the large stove. She was constantly flipping her hair back as it was falling over right her eye.

She took a quick small sip of her wine. She cleared her throat and turned to me, our eyes colliding. "So, what is going on?" She was not the person to beat around the bush. She got right to the point.

I hesitated for a second, trying to gather my thoughts. "Nothing makes sense, this Dori thing, I mean the whole thing, the math, the behavior, all of it..."

After I filled her in on my thoughts, she flatly stated, "Yes, Maxwell, that is exactly it. It makes absolutely no sense but at the time you refused to even discuss the subject." She did seem a bit incredulous that this epiphany of mine took so long.

"Yeah, I know." For a moment, we stood there in silence. Then, I asked her, "So… *What* should I do now?"

She was ready for that question and quickly retorted, "Get a DNA test. That is exactly *what* you should do." She took another drag of her cigarette, seeming a bit frustrated at my apparent trepidation. For her, it was clear what needed to be done, like now.

"How?" I responded sheepishly like I was being politely reprimanded by a professor. My emotions were racing. I felt as if I were questioning this beautiful child of mine, which made me feel sick, disturbed. I kept that feeling to myself. I also knew that my sister was right. The facts were overwhelming. I chose to ignore them.

She knew I was upset and calmed me. She responded, "I will call my primary care doctor and get his recommendation on the best." She continued, "You are doing the right thing here. You have no choice and this is in Dori's best interests and yours, you understand that, right?

I did understand all that she was saying but had difficulty processing it. I felt like I was challenging my baby. It was a horrible feeling. After an hour or so, I left her apartment and continued to my place, which was only a few blocks away.

~

Monday arrived. My sister had been moving quickly. She called me first thing in the morning at my law office. "Maxwell, when is the next time you have the kids?" she asked.

I told her, "Next weekend."

She then inquired, "Can you get them sooner? You need to move, and I need to set the appointment now."

I told her that I would try and would call her back. A part of me wanted to just let this go. I was uneasy about it all. *This must be a bad dream*, I thought. I tried hard to will it out of my mind. That thought was useless. I needed to get to the bottom of this.

The next day I got a call from Collette asking if I could take the kids to their French lesson that Wednesday since she had a conflict. I agreed. I called my sister and alerted her to this fact. Was this some form of divine intervention?

Maggie was blunt. "Then that is the day. Just drop the two the other kids at the lesson and take Dori for the test." I agreed.

I had a sleepless night prior to the test. The darkness and silence that were always enemies of mine gave me comfort that evening for the first time. I don't know why, it just did; quietude was important.

~

Wednesday morning comes with pouring sheets of rain and I arrive at the Lycée Français and wait outside for my kids. After twenty minutes or so, ducking in and out of the entrance door to avoid the pounding downpour, there they appear among the sea of umbrellas with their nanny, heading my way toward the school.

They arrive soaking wet, and they are not happy to go to school. I am nervous and preoccupied with my charge and quickly kiss them all on their cheeks.

Gabriel exclaims, "Why are we going to this stupid school today? It's raining too hard, and we are going to get sick."

I try to calm him while Amara stands there sucking her thumb. The Nanny passes Dori to me and offers me her stroller. I decline.

The Nanny explains to me that she will be back in an hour and a half since their mom wants them right back home following the lesson. That leaves me with little time to do the unthinkable. The clinic is downtown and with the rain and rush hour traffic I am not sure I can get her back on time.

I need to get the two other kids upstairs to the third floor and into their classroom. Getting a taxi is going to be very difficult with the rainy weather and all the commuters heading to their respective destinations vying for a ride.

I get the kids to their classroom and take the stairs back to the lobby, carrying Dori. The elevator is packed. I race toward Madison Avenue with Dori draped across my neck, and am then greeted by the hordes of commuters trying to grab a taxi. Other New Yorkers are huddling and scurrying along the cramped sidewalks, heading to their places of work. The rain is coming down harder now as I cover Dori as best I can with my flimsy black umbrella. We stand by the curb in the rain for what seems like an eternity as I attempt to flag down a driver, a deluge of water pelting the plastic garbage bags at the curb, the street slick black as taxis and cars race by, splashing waves of accumulated rainwater toward us.

Finally, I see out of the corner of my eye a van taxi that is pulling over on the west side of Madison Avenue to drop off a passenger. The light is green with oncoming traffic as I zig-zag across the avenue hustling to grab that fare. As the lady exits the cab, I almost run into her pushing my way into the taxi and apologizing as I slide by her.

She issues a disagreeable stare and says nothing. "I am sorry, but we have an emergency," I blurt out her way as we board the ride. She keeps moving without saying a word.

The trip downtown is a nightmare. Lots of traffic and nothing is moving. My anxiety kicks in. I am soaked and sweating profusely, sitting in that cab as it is halted in traffic. Dori rolls around on the seat in a playful way. She's jumping up and down, laughing and hugging me, only increasing my stress.

As we approach 42nd Street, it is clear we are not going to make it to the clinic and get back on time. I ask the cab driver to pull over, pay him, grab Dori, exit the car and rush toward the subway at Grand Central Station. I descend the stairs to the subway platform, and I am greeted by the throngs of commuters jockeying for position to board the train.

I force my way onto the train, holding Dori tight to my chest. We are jammed up against the door, squeezed tightly amid the soaked passengers. We get off the train at the Union Square 14th street station, race up the stairs and onto the street. The rain has slowed down as I scurry two blocks south to where the medical clinic is located. I look at my phone and see that almost forty minutes had gone by from the start of this hellish journey.

I am trembling and feeling sick. All the way to the downtown spot I'm questioning this wonderment in my life. A betrayal of my daughter. I hate every minute of it. When we arrive at the medical office, I see that the clinic is located on the first floor and we enter the room.

The clinic is packed and depressing with no windows, dirty white walls, stained gray carpeting, metal chairs lined up in rows and a musty smell that is pungent. I sit there among the rain-soaked crowd thinking, *No way is this going to work.* Time is running out.

Dori starts to cry. She is on my lap and off my lap as she is becoming irritable. I shake so badly that the person next to me, a nice young woman, walks up to the front of the line and alerts the nurse. The nurse comes over to me and asks if I am okay. I am not and she allows me to go to see the doctor ahead of the line.

I cannot fill out the forms. My hands are shaking too much. I am desperately trying to hold back tears. The nurse is kind enough to fill everything out for me.

I find the strength to get through this horrible ordeal. I repeat to myself, *This is not of my making. My intent is to protect my daughter and nothing else.* You can surprise yourself with the untapped power you have in difficult times, and I learned on that day to tap it.

The doctor arrives and takes two swabs of my daughter's nose and mine. That is it. That is the test.

We get out of there and make it back to the Nanny. She is standing there outside the school with the other two children. She does not ask me any questions, but I know she thinks something is up. We part and I head back to my apartment.

~

I sat in my apartment thinking of Dori and why such a young child needed to be called into question like that and I felt terrible. My intentions were pure. I wanted to raise a family and be happy. I did not invite this into our lives. I thought of Mary and how young she was when she got sick. I found strength in that reflection. It calmed me.

I remember that prior to her diagnosis she was always crying and seemed generally miserable. I pictured my mother trying to soothe her, but it was of no use. I would sometimes approach her for a hug or ask her to play. Most times I got rebuffed. She would peer up at me with her tiny face that had freckles on her nose and around her eyes, Irish pale skin and soft blue eyes and in very harsh tones tell me to go away. She seemed really upset at me and I had no clue as to why.

She was a baby in a constant state of agitation. I remember seeing that my mother was confused about her behavior. Her attempts to console Mary rarely worked so she allowed her to let these periods of discomfort, or more precisely tantrums, run their course. There was nothing else she could do, so I thought.

I remember my mother noticing that my sister developed black and blue marks that would suddenly appear on different parts of her small frame. My parents had no idea why these marks would appear on her body. I would hear my mom talking to my dad saying that maybe she got these black and blues playing outside. She would tell my father that maybe she is injury prone.

Our family doctor suggested that Mary go to the hospital to get blood work done. The diagnosis was leukemia. I could not understand why a baby would be diagnosed with such a horrible disease. It made no sense to me since she was so young.

Mary's disease caused her to be in a lot of pain. She was constantly with my mother and as the weeks and months passed, she would appear back from the hospital following her chemotherapy and radiation treatment looking more and more changed. Her hair became thinner and thinner until it fell out completely. She wore a bandana. Her face became puffy and red from all the prednisone shots she was getting from the doctor. Her mood was mercurial. One moment she would seem happy and the next she would get mad and just cry for no reason.

I remember trying to cuddle her sometimes, but she did not like that. She would recoil and push me away. That did not stop me since I wanted so much to comfort her and make her laugh. So, I started to give her all kinds of nicknames that would come into my head. I called her Dinky Junior. I think she liked that nickname.

As the disease progressed, she became more disturbed and upset and I saw needle marks all over her. My mom explained to me that the doctors would need to find other areas of her body to inject medicine since the veins in her arms were too damaged and bruised from the constant injections. Her immune system became totally compromised and she would get sick a lot with strange diseases like shingles.

She lived in my parents' bedroom most of the time when she wasn't in the hospital. I would see her lying in my mother's single bed. Many times, I could hear her crying or on occasion yelling, saying all kinds of wild stuff sometimes directed at my mom or dad. I couldn't make out what she was saying but I could tell it was not nice. I periodically would peer unnoticed into the bedroom and see her on the bed as my mother would place warm compresses on her back while saying the rosary. My father would tell me to close the door and I would retreat to my bedroom on the third floor to hear Mary's screaming and yelling continue for long periods at a time. I was scared as I laid in bed.

When it was time to bathe her, my mother had to be careful. Her skin was falling off her back. I saw my mom trying to reconnect the skin with oils and bandages. Then she would carry Mary to the bathroom and slowly place her in the tub. My mom once asked me to prepare her bath ahead of time and to put some holy water into the bath water. I did it. When my sister was placed into the bath water, she let out the most horrifying screams once the water touched her body. I bit my nails as I nervously watched this all happen.

As time went on Mary spent more and more of her life at the hospital. My dad was traveling a lot so my mother would spend many nights on a cot in the hospital room with my sister.

~

On my birthday, November 1, 2007, I arrived at my apartment, and prior to heading to the elevator I decided to check my mailbox. I was eagerly awaiting these DNA results and knew they would arrive any day. I left my reading glasses at work, but upon opening the small mailbox I saw a letter from that medical office. I opened the letter but could not read a thing since the print font was miniscule.

A young guy was next to me, thirtyish or so, checking his mail and I politely asked, "I am sorry, I left my glasses at work, can you tell me what that says?"

He was much shorter than me and sort of stared up as our eyes met. He was hesitant at first and then asked, "What is it?"

I responded, "A test result."

"You sure?" he said, his voice equivocal, unsure. I knew I put him on the spot but my anxiousness to know right then and there was driving me.

I handed him the one-page letter. He looked at it for a moment and I could see his face change. He stared up at me, handed the note back, and said, "I'm sorry."

I thanked him and raced toward the elevator. I still could not believe this was true.

When I got into my apartment I found a pair of reading glasses, sat on the red sofa and read the findings. I saw seven doctors had signed off on the report which contained a series of numerical entries, listed side by side, that did not match. Peering further down the document I saw the finding, a 'zero percent likelihood' that my daughter was mine.

I stared at the document, reading it repeatedly in total disbelief. I was shocked at the results. I never truly thought until the minute I saw it, that Dori was not my biological daughter.

I got up and paced the room with uncontrollable thoughts whipping through my mind. *This can't be true, this is crazy...* I called my sister Maggie and told her what the report said. She was silent for a second; I could feel while she thought this might be the case, it was a shock to her too. After a long pause, she blurted out, "Come over as soon as you can."

I had no words, and replied, "Okay."

I left my apartment and went to her place. She opened the door and without saying a word hustled into the kitchen. She was disturbed by it all. The fan went on, and she lit up a cigarette.

"Are you surprised? I am not. It's still unbelievable to learn this but I am not surprised." She took another drag, turned her head on an angle to aim the smoke up the fan. "I mean, by the way are you okay?" And before I could respond, she abruptly stated, "This is not a surprise, we all thought this was a possibility."

I asked her, "What do I do now?" I was still trying to grasp what had come crashing down into my life.

She poured wine into my glass. "If you want a cigarette, just make sure you blow it up at the fan, so the kids won't smell it."

I declined.

"Maxwell, you need to tell her and… Wait, do you have a lawyer?"

I responded, "No."

"You need one now," she told me firmly.

She asked if she could read the report. I handed it to her, and she looked at it shaking her head in total disbelief. She then looked at me straight in the eye, and said, "I am not surprised. Maxwell, this is what I thought and many others the whole time. I am sorry but the truth is better than not knowing. You will get through this. You are protecting your daughter, so know that. Be strong." I was silent and just listened. She then asked me, "When are you going to tell Collette about this?"

A brief silence ensued between us. My mind was racing. Hers too, so I thought. "I don't know, what do you think?"

"Now, is what I think," she responded fiercely. I could tell she was stunned by the whole thing as she fidgeted with her hair.

I walked around the kitchen thinking and thinking and then stated, "I need some time to calm down a bit, this changes everything. I just can't believe this, this deception, this lie is incredible."

"Are you kidding me?" she retorted, pacing back and forth, clutching the report. "Incredible, it's outrageous. Call her now."

My sister was not one to wait for anything. She wanted things to move on the spot. I hesitated for a second and said, "No, not yet. I don't even have a lawyer. I need one now. I have no idea what this will mean legally. I have to understand my rights." She reluctantly agreed as I saw her becoming increasingly disturbed.

We both moved to the living room and sat in total silence. I could tell she was trying to process this as well. "Okay, today, I mean now you need to get a lawyer, okay?"

I agreed.

"Okay, do you need help getting one?"

"No, let me go back to my law office and think."

"Okay, but call me later, all right. Hang in there."

We moved to the entrance, she gave me a hug, and I left.

~

That night I dream of my mother. We walk along my childhood beach, side by side. She no longer inhabits a wheelchair and is acting playful toward me as we view the waves crashing on the shore. She is younger and the world around us is bright, and we feel joyful as we play at the edges of the ocean line. It's then that my mother turns to me with the brightest smile, takes my hand, and we dance, our feet together submerged in the water to the sound of her childhood music. She shows me the steps she grew up with as a young girl in the 1940s. Her big brown eyes shining against the bright blue sea. She is so happy to be with me in this private moment.

~

The next day I went to see a close law colleague of mine. When I peered into his office, he looked up, smiled, and invited me in. He was a seasoned attorney in his mid-sixties and had the biggest, whitest teeth I have ever seen. When he smiled, it was like a blinding light coming right at you.

"What's up, Maxwell, everything okay?" he said as he looked down, fumbling his fingers through some heavy insurance treatise he was reading, and looked up from the book. He was a bright guy, and he was an insurance law teacher at Fordham Law School. "Sit down. Relax. You look stressed as hell." He then motioned his hands. "Talk, what's going on?" He looked at me, our eyes now met.

I hesitated for a second and then explained the whole situation. He was nonplussed and immediately offered up the name of a lawyer that he knew and thought very highly of. He gave me his contact information and I called him straight away from my office.

His secretary put me right through to him, Bill Langford. I explained what was happening and to my surprise he asked if I could come over right away. His office was only blocks from where I worked so off I went with a check stuffed in my wallet.

When I arrived, I was ushered by his secretary into his office. He got up, introduced himself and asked if I would like something to drink. I said, "Water will be fine." He called his secretary and moments later a bottle of water arrived.

Bill was a tall man, fifty-something, handsome, and dressed impeccably in a gray suit. He looked at me, smiled, and quietly asked, "So, tell me what's happening." He then leaned back in his chair and folded his arms behind his neck.

I explained the history of the case. The details of the divorce complaint she served me at my office in April 2007. I then handed him the DNA report. He took a quick look at the report, and then leaned forward, his elbows resting on his desk, stared at me and asked, "How are you doing?"

"I have no clue. This is nuts," I blurted out.

He smiled and then got right to the matter at hand. "I know this lawyer who is representing your wife." He paused for a moment and then said, "He is an expert in international divorce law. He is an expert on the Hague Convention which comes into play in these types of situations." He continued. "The French are tricky. They are, believe it or not, very litigious, and most times want to return to their country, especially in divorce situations. They got this fascination with the United States, but over time they simply are drawn back to their land. That's not to say she can just leave. Under New York Family law, she has a ninety-mile radius from the custodial dwelling on where she can move, that's the law."

He closely observed me and then in a very calm but direct manner gave me a critical piece of information that I had never thought of. "But, with these folks *you* got to be careful, they can get desperate and pull all kinds of stuff on you to find a legal reason to leave. Like try to bankrupt you, you hearing me?"

I just kept listening, numb now with that bit of intelligence. As Bill spoke my mind drifted some as I thought to myself how incredible this whole thing was. *I mean, here I am sitting with a divorce lawyer who's telling me all this terrible stuff about what the woman I married will likely try to pull on me. I married this person, for Christ's sake, had kids with her, and slept in the same bed with her.* It was disturbing to be there in this office with that man telling me she would do anything to hurt me.

His office was huge, and pictures of his kids were everywhere. I could tell he was divorced. It was obvious with all the pictures of a very attractive woman many years younger than him prominently displayed on his credenza and elsewhere in his office.

I stared at the numerous pictures of him and some prominent people that he must have represented in their divorces. One character was well known, a billionaire financier. His divorce was all over the papers for quite some time. I thought, *How the hell am I going to afford him?*

I kept studying the pictures, as he spoke in his confident manner. I was thinking as I glanced at all the pictures, and thought, *This is like the who's who of the New York elite, what am I doing here?*

He continued. "He is a good lawyer but a prick. He likes to drag things out, pit one party against the other, churn things up, you know what I mean?"

This download was hard for me to process. I retorted, "Yes, I got it. So, what do you think?" What else is there to say.

Bill was abundantly clear and I was being schooled. "You seem a little distracted."

"Um... No. I am fine. Just a little stressed by all this."

He nodded to say he understood and pressed forward with the meeting. "We need to get in touch with him right away and advise him of this, this is a game changer. But that does not mean even with this discovery we will not be in for a battle."

He stopped and thought for a second. He then clicked his pen and scribbled some notes on a yellow legal pad. "By the way, did you ever have an affair during your marriage to her?" That woke me up.

I thought for a moment and said, "No," although I thought to myself, I wished I had.

"By the way, are you paying her money right now?"

"Yes," I said, thinking I had made a mistake.

He shook his head. "Well, stop for now until we get a meeting set. Nothing, Nada."

I agreed, not knowing at all what to say.

"When do you see the kids next?"

"This coming weekend."

"Okay, well do not discuss this with her, say *nothing* to her, got it?"

I nodded yes.

He then got up from his huge, ornate mahogany desk and moved to his small but well-organized conference table. All his papers perfectly arranged and labeled. I was waiting for the money talk now.

He paused and then stated, "So, I know Chuck, great guy. He spoke highly of you and really thought I would be your best guy to handle this. I get aggressive and her lawyer knows my reputation. I also have very good relationships with the judges in family court." I continued to listen. He then changed course. "You a litigator?"

I blurted back, "I was years back a securities litigator but then moved into corporate."

He leaned back in his chair, looked up at the ceiling and then laughed a little. "Well, you guys aren't cheap, and your firm, well, they have a healthy rate."

I agreed and waited for the financial bomb to come down. I felt he was leading me into this and all I could think of was sticker shock.

"So", he said, "I know Chuck and Chuck wants me to handle your divorce. That's a good thing. I only like client references from folks I trust, and Chuck is one of them. Celebrity types, and I handle lots of those situations, are a different thing, you know what I mean. Great fees and marketing, of course."

I was waiting. I knew the financial gavel was about to fall. I braced myself.

"Okay, let's talk about next steps, then money, you good with that?"

"Yes."

"Steps: right now, I need to get this information in her lawyer's hand and then set up a meeting with all of us. I will review the complaint she filed against you and think through what they are going to try to pull here." He quickly asked, "Oh, I forgot; no, arrests, claims of domestic abuse right, clean record?"

"Yes. Nothing of that sort."

"Good, good." He continued, "This type of stuff can get crazy, so be prepared. I mean, the stuff she is going to say about you, trust me: awful. It's he-said-she-said kind of thing, but that can drag stuff out. The money is the focus. Always has been, always will be. Greed."

Without me responding, he went right into the money. "So, Maxwell, let's say a fifteen-thousand-dollar retainer, now my rate is nine hundred dollars per hour but I will, because I know Chuck, take this process though the next two months without time charging, just the flat fee retainer amount and then we will assess where we are and what's ahead of us, you okay with that?"

I was relieved. "Yes, absolutely. So, you will handle this?" Before he could respond, I was gushing with thanks and more thanks, and I could tell his ego was elevated. I cut the check and signed the retainer agreement that was prepared in advance of my arrival.

I left and headed back to my office. As I walked back, I wanted so badly to just call her and say, *You're caught.* One thing I thought about, as I did when the results first arrived at my apartment, was that all the confusion for so long about her behavior. Her actions now came into clear focus.

That felt good. At least I was not crazy.

~

A week later Bill advised me that he had spoken to her counsel. He stated that her lawyer would have a talk with her and then suggested we all get together at his office for a meeting.

I asked, "Well, was he blown away?"

"No, Maxwell. These things, I know this is huge for you and it should be, but they are not rare. No, he simply stated what I said, that's it. Also, when we do meet, be prepared for an attack on you. No apologies, no, she will be prepared. He will prepare her. She will be emotionless."

I didn't know. Divorce law is its own world.

So, Thanksgiving arrived and no meeting yet. My lawyer was explaining that they kept pushing the dates out. I said, "Why? Bill, I have not given her any money this month. I mean, wouldn't she want to get into a room now?"

"Maxwell," he responded, "who knows? Maybe the biological father is paying her money. Trust me, her lawyer is going to pull something. He is great at that.

Try not to speculate—this is divorce. Do your best to *not* be emotional, she is going to be coached, okay?"

I thought while listening to him, how foreign this all was to me. *I have no clue.*

~

I had the kids over the Thanksgiving holiday, and we all went to my brother Joe's house. He has three girls, and all the kids were roughly the same age. It was a nice getaway—clear the head.

That Wednesday, I picked up the kids at her place. She answered the door. "Hi. How are you?"

I was thinking to myself, *Are you kidding me, with what I just learned.* She was cool as a cucumber. "The kids are coming down now. I hope you all enjoy the Thanksgiving holiday."

The kids all came stumbling down the steps with their backpacks. Their bags had already been packed and were right in the foyer. I wanted to say something so badly to her but refrained based upon my lawyer's advice. I wished her a great Thanksgiving and headed out of the city to my brother's place in New Jersey about an hour away.

The ride out was a great distraction. The kids were so excited to see their cousins and Uncle Joe was their favorite uncle. He and his wife were always planning things like pumpkin patch tours, ice skating, and anything else they could find that was fun.

When we arrived, his three kids came running out of the house to greet my little ones. In a second they all dispersed and the fun for them began. Joe pulled me aside and stated in disbelief, "Holy cow, that news is crazy. Maggie shared it all. Just relax, man, how do you feel?"

I didn't want to get into it, so I said politely, "Fine. Joe, it answered a lot of questions for me." We left it at that.

The long weekend was great. The kids were having a blast and a lot of football was watched and martinis poured. At some point, I got a call from Collette who asked to speak to the kids and wish them a happy Thanksgiving.

I thought for a second but could not help myself.

I asked, "Collette, have you met with your lawyer yet?"

She responded, "Yes."

Nothing else but yes was said. I thought, Man, Bill must be right. She is like ice, no emotion.

I continued with some hesitation in my voice, "Is there *anything* you want to talk about?

"No," she replied in a manner that suggested what would there to be to talk about.

I felt like an idiot at this point but kept going. "Well, *you* know, right?"

"What?"

"So, *you* spoke to your lawyer, right?"

Again, a pithy, "Yes."

"Is there *anything* you would like to tell me?"

She calmly said, "No."

I felt she was dumbfounded by why I would even ask her these questions. I was feeling stupid at this point but then I thought of Bill's words at his office that day: "She will be coached very well."

I knew Bill would not want me to have any discussion like this, but I needed to know. "So, *you* have nothing to say about what your lawyer told you?"

Again, "No."

I went silent. I had nothing to say. This woman was not going to offer me anything. I was stunned. "Okay. I will put the kids on." That was it.

When I got back to New York I dropped the kids off. She answered the door, asked if we had fun and ushered the kids upstairs. I said goodbye and left.

~

Christmas 2007 arrived and still no meeting or word from the other side. I was becoming increasingly perplexed by the whole thing. I just did not get that with this bunker buster discovery why her side would not be rushing to the table to get something done.

Bill was firm with me. "Cool it. It will happen. Don't rush it. They know the deal. Trust me. This is a game."

The holiday season ended and on January 4th Bill received a call from her lawyer. They both agreed to a meeting at her lawyer's office on January 11th.

I thought, *Finally, after all these months, we can now sit down and sort this out.* I called Bill and we had a long discussion about the meeting and what I should expect. One of the things I made clear was that I wanted the identity of the biological father. That was of paramount importance to me. Bill seemed pretty confident they would offer up his identity, but he made clear to me that it would come with a price.

"Price, what does that mean?" I exclaimed.

Bill was very matter of fact. "They are not going to offer up his identity for nothing."

I sat back in my office chair, staring out of the window that gave me a clear view of the MetLife Building, remembering that when I was young it was called the Pan Am Building, not knowing what to say next.

I quickly gathered my thoughts. "Okay, Bill. I mean, are we not entitled to this information as a matter of law? I mean the level of deception here is huge. A judge would see this, right? And order it?"

A few seconds of silence ensued on Bill's end and then politely but firmly he replied, "Maxwell, a judge could *not* care less. His only concern—and please get this—is the *best interests* of the child, nothing more, and then setting down a child support payment. You are getting way too personal. I don't blame you but the reality is family courts only care about the welfare of the child. The rest is of no importance here. You get that?"

I hesitated for a moment trying to digest what Bill had just said. "Well, okay but I feel we are being held hostage here, you know? This is a child we are talking about."

Bill quickly interjected. "Maxwell, the judge wants to know one thing regarding Dori and that is do you plan to adopt her?"

"Yes, of course, I want to adopt her."

"Then, great, we can mention that when we meet with the other side."

"Okay," I said. I was done. I thought, *Just go with it, you're clueless.*

Bill then gave me the time and address. "Be there a half hour early, so we can go over a few things, get you calm before we meet them. So, say around nine-thirty a.m. in front of their building, 225 Madison Avenue?"

"Yes, see you then, Bill, and thanks."

"Maxwell, chin up—see you then."

~

January 11th arrived. I was a bit nervous. I had no idea what to expect. I got there at nine-thirty. Bill arrived five minutes later. We stood out in front of the building and Bill went through a few ground rules with me.

"Maxwell, remember this guy, her lawyer is going to attack you, your character. So, be calm, say nothing. Just sit down and let me handle it. Got it?"

"Yes."

"Okay, good. Now, did you bring a check with you?"

"Of course. By the way, how much are they going to want for this information? Man, Bill, this is like blackmail to me."

Bill thought for a second, smiled, and said, "You are right, it is." He then quickly followed up with, "Legal blackmail, unfortunately." I was ready and off we went to her lawyer's office.

We got up to the floor and we entered the waiting area. I was very surprised. The office was beaten up. A small, dingy waiting area. Brown, stained carpeting that looked like it hadn't been replaced in decades. The receptionist was sitting behind a thick piece of glass that reminded me of the glass you would see at the prisons where I used to work. The walls had old, torn wallpaper. The chairs were frayed in places and the room was windowless and dimly lit. The only source of light were these cheap lamps that rested on a few scratched side tables. I thought, *This is the fancy lawyer's office.*

The receptionist finally came out and escorted us to a conference room where through the glass window panel I caught a glimpse of Collette and her lawyer sitting there waiting for us. We entered and right away, as Bill predicted, I was greeted by her lawyer. He was a short, stout, roundish figure, balding and red faced with huge glasses that covered most of his face. His suit looked cheap. It was shiny.

As we entered, he immediately stood up and instead of shaking hands, leaned over the table and exclaimed, almost shouted at me with his chubby finger pointed right in my face, "You are a deadbeat father!"

I was stunned at his remark and reacted right away. "What? Fuck you!"

Bill jumped in right away and instructed me to sit down and be quiet. I was perplexed and wanted to tear this guy's head off. Things simmered down and Bill started the meeting.

"Bob, let's relax and try to get something done here today." Her lawyer mumbled something inaudible to me and sat back down. I looked over at Collette sitting there between her lawyer and the paralegal that was brought into the meeting. She was silent but would periodically glance at the paralegal with a slight childish smirk on her face. We said nothing to each other.

"So, Bob, my client wants to get the biological situation resolved today."

Bob shot back, "Like what?"

Bill leaned back in his chair and calmly stated, "He wants his identity."

Bob glanced at Collette and then turned toward Bill and firmly stated, "Well, we want money now. It's been almost two months since my client was paid anything. So, let's talk cash." I was thinking, *What the fuck, they went deep for two months—not us. This guy is an asshole.*

I periodically looked at Collette. She was coached and appeared like a total stranger to me. I thought, *This is my wife, the woman I married and had kids with.* I could not believe it. She had no emotion, nothing—she was this alien figure sitting across the conference room table from me. *A woman I married and now, an adversary,* I thought.

Bill then stated, "Well, the child support discussion will come later. This, Bob. This needs to be handled now."

Bob immediately shot back, "So, is he planning on adopting the child?"

I jumped in, angry. "Yes, counselor, that is correct. What do you think?"

I looked at Collette and she had no reaction. She and the paralegal kept making eye contact with each other, exchanging little giggles and smirks. I felt like this was a game to her. I wanted to jump across the table and shake her up.

Bill then asked that we take a five minute break. Bob agreed and we left the conference room and quietly discussed what to do next.

"Maxwell, you see what's happening right?

I responded, "Yes. It's crazy, Bill, her lawyer is a jerk."

Bill tried to focus me now, get me calmer with less emotion. "He is paid to be. Relax. I told you this would be the case. Remember, so let's get this done."

"Bill, what do they want?"

He thought for a minute, and asked me, "What can you pay right now, you have your check right?"

"Yes, so what is the number?"

Bill thought and said, "Around ten thousand."

"What!" I exclaimed. "This is nuts. This is totally crazy. I feel like she is wrong here and now I am paying for it."

Bill stated fiercely, "Maxwell, this is a game. I have explained all this to you. You want the identity or what? Her lawyer is probably thinking more money than that. Can we go back in there and make the offer, yes, or no?

"Yes," I said, overwhelmingly frustrated. I just could not believe this was how it would go.

We then went back in the room and Bill made the offer. Her lawyer began to haggle a bit but then said, "Well, if that is it—fine. However, we want the money today, now."

Bill looked at me. I pulled my check out and wrote it. Bill then followed with, "We want the identity *now*."

Her lawyer retorted "You will have his name first thing in the morning, Bill, trust me."

I was uneasy about this deal. I looked at Bill and he shook his head, confirming to me to take it. I did and then we all abruptly departed. When we got to the street Bill explained that all was good.

"Maxwell, this is a process but at least you will get closure on this biological father issue and then we will go from there. I know you are frustrated but divorce is not easy, and your wife is remorseless, let me tell you. This is her now, you got to get used to it."

We parted and I went back to my office stunned at what had just happened. I thought of our marriage, the kids. Everything was flying through my mind. *And it all comes down to this, money, strangers now going at it.*

~

The next morning, I arrived at my office at around seven in the morning. I turned my computer on and saw an email from Collette that came to me last night. I quickly opened it, and it read, 'I thought about the whole thing. I cannot reveal his name to you. He is married with three children, and I can't be responsible for destroying his marriage.'

I was shocked. I read the email maybe five times. *She duped me*, so I thought. I immediately called my bank and asked if the check had been cashed yet. The representative on the other end asked me the amount, put me on hold and then confirmed that it had been cashed yesterday afternoon.

I shouted back to her, "You got to stop it! It's a fraud!"

She responded. "It's too late but I'll put you over to our fraud division for assistance." I said no and hung up.

It was too early to call Bill. I just sat at my desk fuming at the whole thing. I thought, *Blackmail, yes, and a total thief too.*

That day, I tried to get Bill on the phone. His secretary kept insisting that he was in court and would return my call probably after five. Bill, oddly enough, did not call me back that day. I was perplexed. The next day and for several days to come I tried to get him on the phone but to no avail.

I visited with Chuck and explained what was going on. He was surprised but advised me to hold tight. I did, begrudgingly.

Weeks passed and no Bill. My messages turned into pleas begging him to call me back. Not a word.

I finally gave up; went to see Chuck and he was very surprised too. He said, "Fire him and get as much money back as you can. This is not good, and I am sorry I introduced him to you. I mean, he has a great reputation." I agreed but felt I was vulnerable now.

I then spent another two weeks or so trying to get him on the phone to let him know I was done. I couldn't even get him on the phone to fire him. This whole thing was embarrassing and upsetting.

Finally, he called me from the courthouse, and I let him have it. "I've been trying to get you for weeks. What the hell? This is crazy. I don't even have the name of the father. I spent ten grand to get it. Where have you been?"

He was silent for a second and said, "Maybe you should get new counsel." He fired me. I demanded my money back and he then said, "Well, most is spent on preparation, meetings, review of the pleadings. And by the way, it was a flat fee."

This had turned into a nightmare. I had no words. I thought, *Not only am I in the midst of an ugly divorce with my wife, now I am in the process of a divorce with my lawyer.* I knew that her lawyer was out for the kill, and I lost my captain. I was easy prey, so I thought.

I went back into Chuck's office and explained my conversation with Bill.

Chuck rolled his eyes, smiled at me, and said, "Maxwell, get what you can back and move on. You got bigger things to deal with and this time, get a woman to represent you. I am sorry. Bill is an excellent lawyer but probably concluded that you did not have the financial stuff to go the distance. He is crazy expensive. You were low on his ecosystem."

I shot back, "Chuck, I don't care who he represents. He dumped me. He took my money. He should be reported to the Bar Association. This is unethical."

Chuck tried to calm me and bring some reality into this. "Maxwell, the last thing you want is to report Bill and get into that while you're dealing with an ugly divorce. Just get what you can and move on. I have been through divorce myself and it was ugly too. It was expensive, emotional, and a nightmare. Men get screwed." He continued, "I know a woman attorney, a lot cheaper, more flexible and excellent. I am sorry I didn't refer you to her the first time. I just thought Bill was tough and with his reputation he would scare your wife's lawyer. Here, I have her card. Call her. And put Bill to bed."

I had nothing to say. I wasn't upset at Chuck. I was lost. I stared at her card and agreed. I then went to my office and got Bill on the phone, and he agreed to give me back five thousand.

At this point, I did not even care. I was beaten up and the fight had not started yet.

I studied the new lawyer's business card. Her name was Judy Hemp and I thought hopefully she could help me. I mean, I felt naked and totally exposed to the enemy. I thought, *This is a war and I am running around the battlefield without a gun.*

I called Judy and I was put through to her office. She had a soothing voice and asked if I was available to come over right away. I hopped in a taxi and fled to her office.

~

When I got off the elevator I was surprised by how beautiful her firm looked: all white marble, beautiful modern paintings, soft white leather sofas, and very nice receptionists. The law firm reminded me of some high-powered movie agency in Hollywood, like you would see in a film.

I was escorted to her office, and it was equally stunning, resting on the thirty-fifth floor, a large corner office with panoramic views of the city. She was a young, attractive woman with pictures of her kids and husband all over the place: bright, cheery, and soothing, so I felt.

When I entered, she smiled, introduced herself, and asked me to sit down. I explained the Bill situation and then gave her an overview of the entire divorce. She listened intently, shaking her head up and down periodically as she scribbled down notes. When I finished my account of this nightmare that was unfolding, she sat back, thought for a moment in silence, leaned forward and methodically walked me through her strategy.

"Maxwell, you seem to want the identity of the biological father. Is that true?"

I said, "Yes."

She then softly and in a very calm manner observed, "I know his identity is important to you. However, to get that information we would have to sue for it and have good cause to get a court to agree to order the release of that information. That would be expensive and a long process. Also, Maxwell, the chances of the court ordering it would be remote. They simply don't care. They are only interested in the best interests of your children. That's it. The biological issue to a judge means nothing. I am sorry but these judges deal with a lot of crazy situations and their caseload is overwhelming. So, my suggestion is that we deal with trying to get this settled without court intervention, and then revisit this issue. Please trust me on this."

I began to feel better. I felt her truthfulness and sincerity. She then moved right to the engagement terms. *No bullshit here,* I thought. She was a matter of fact and right to the point. I liked that. "If you want to move forward with me, as your lawyer, I will require a small retainer, say, seven thousand five hundred dollars, and will bill out at a discounted rate for you. Does that seem fair?"

I was ready to go. "Yes, absolutely," I responded.

She called her assistant into her office and explained the fee arrangement and within five minutes he came back in with the engagement that I reviewed, signed, and cut the check. We talked for a little while longer about logistics and she explained she would enter her appearance as my counsel, contact the other side, and we would then meet to go over next steps. I thanked her profusely and left.

~

When I got to the street I thought, why not go see the kids, I know they are out of school at the playground right near the house.

I first called Maggie who was aware of the Bill debacle. She was relieved and happy that I had retained a new lawyer. She was especially delighted that it was a woman. I agreed and thanked her for all her support.

After I got off the phone with Maggie, I took a cab over to see them, entered the playground, and saw my girls playing on the swings while Gabriel was navigating the jungle gym. I saw the Nanny pushing Dori on the baby swing as she screamed, "Higher, higher!" Amara was dangling on her swing, sucking her thumb as usual. The place was packed with kids screaming and running all over the place, basketball games were going on next to the playground and nannies were feeding kids, while others were chasing them around the playground.

When I arrived, I snuck up on the girls. Amara hopped off the swing and jumped right into my arms as Dori continued to be pushed by the Nanny on the swing. I kissed and hugged Amara and blew a kiss Dori's way, and then marched with Amara to see Gabriel who was about to launch himself down the sliding board.

Our eyes met as I got closer to the jungle gym and he went nuts, flung himself on to the sliding board, and jumped off running my way yelling, "Papa!" his arms flailing. We all played together for almost two hours. It felt good to see the kids like this. A surprise visit and not some pre-arranged pick-up, which had become the normal course. For the first time in a while, I felt joyful and managed to brush aside all the craziness of the recent divorce events.

The kids, exhausted now, begged me to go to the house for a while so we could continue to play. I agreed and off we went. Being with the kids like this gave me such a great feeling. We were all happy.

When we arrived at the house, we raced together up to the third floor and played. I hadn't been to their home in so long and the various familiar surroundings hit me all at once. I felt nostalgic. I became emotional as I peered at various familiar things that brought back memories of an earlier time with the kids that seemed so long ago. *Time really does pass quickly*, I thought.

I also noticed that every picture of me either alone or taken with me and the kids was gone. There was no trace of me in the home where I lived for so many years. It was a strange feeling to think how fast you can be erased from someone's life, without a thought.

We all continued to play and watch some cartoons on the television. It was a blast. I felt human. I thought this was one of the best days for me in a long time.

~

March 2008 arrived and the legal games and anything else that she and her lawyer could come up with to stick it to me were in full throttle.

I remember every time I would pick the kids up for a weekend, or holiday, I would be greeted by Collette. I would plead with her to back her lawyer off, sit down with me and get to some sort of resolution.

I was clear. "Collette, you are bankrupting the bank. Do you understand that? If this continues, we will go broke."

Her response was the exact same each time, "Talk to your lawyer."

I could not get through to her. She was unrecognizable to me now. I never anticipated this happening.

Then, she pulled a move that woke me up and led me to go hard. I was at my apartment and received a phone call from Judy. "Are you sitting down?" she asked.

I said, "What, what is going on now?"

"I got a call from her lawyer, and he said, and I quote, 'Unless you support Dori, you will never see her again'."

I was done. It was wrong. I came to know with a divorce all bets are off. I did not know that someone, here my soon to be ex-wife, would put a child in the middle of this debacle.

Judy tried to calm me. "Maxwell, I am sorry but your wife and that lawyer are impossible."

"But, Judy, when did I ever say I would not support Dori? I made that clear in her lawyer's office back in January. I love her. I thought I adopted her already, for Christ's sake. Why would this even be brought up? It makes no sense."

"I agree," she responded.

"Well, did you tell her lawyer that?"

"I did."

"Good, what did he say?"

"He said that he would talk to your wife about it."

Then, Judy dropped another bomb on me. "He also stated that she intends to pursue sole custody."

I needed to sit down for this one. My head was spinning. I remained silent for a second or two, trying to salvage any composure that I could muster. "What, are you kidding me, based on what," I exclaimed.

Judy responded fiercely, "Maxwell, it is crazy, she has no basis whatsoever. These are tactics to get more money out of you or make a play to leave for France, that's it. It's dirty but so is divorce."

I had to ask, "But, Judy, is this something you have come across in divorce matters? It's nuts."

"Maxwell," she stated with utter conviction, "this wife of yours wants out of this country period. I believe that her lawyer is an expert on making this type of thing happen. I know her attorney will stop at nothing but ultimately, it is her call on these matters. This is a new one for me. I can only say I am sorry. But, that said, Maxwell we got to go hard now."

"Well," I responded firmly, "don't you believe the judge will see right through this and hold them accountable for this frivolous nonsense? What I mean, Judy, is sanction them for such outrageous behavior."

"Yes, he will find this latest demand crazy since there is no evidence in the record to warrant such a harsh remedy that they appear to be seeking, but the problem is that once they make the motion, if they do, it will have to be litigated which will take months and tremendous legal cost."

I sighed in complete disbelief at this new turn of events. I was lost at this point. I was angry but knew my anger would get me nowhere. Somewhat defeated at this point I simply pointed out to Judy, "I have no idea why they are playing games this way, Judy. I am done. This nonsense is over. You understand?"

I could feel her sense of compassion on the other end of the phone. "I get it, Maxwell, I truly do."

I could also detect that Judy sensed I was blaming her in part. "Judy, I am aware this has nothing to do with you. I think, at this point, we need to go hard. You have done a great job. This just needs to end now."

I knew we were scheduled for a court appearance that Monday, and I wanted my lawyer to file every motion possible to nail them to the wall. I told Judy, "You file everything and anything to fuck them up."

I also made clear to Judy that I was going to put together a list of settlement demands and if they played games with any of them, we would just see them in court. I knew, and Judy agreed, that the family court judge would be pretty upset at all the nonsense that they threw our way.

We were well documented in our efforts to reach a fair settlement.

As Judy said, "The last thing they want is to go to court. So, I agree, Maxwell. Let's throw everything we got at them with your demands."

"Yes, Judy, and twenty-four hours to accept or we just appear before the judge."

That night I listed my demands and emailed them to Judy. She was on the phone with me that morning, which was a Friday, and the court appearance was coming up Monday morning. She agreed with my demands and sent them straight away to Collette's attorney stating, "Your client has twenty-four hours to accept the terms, or we file what we need to and see you in court."

That Saturday night, I received a call from Collette. I was cold but remained calm.

"Maxwell," she said, "I reviewed your documents, and it seems fair so I will agree to it."

I quickly and coldly responded, "Have your lawyer put that into writing to my lawyer." She agreed she would and on Sunday morning my lawyer had the confirmation.

The case was finally over. It was May 2008. We signed the separation agreement on September 17, 2008 and the divorce decree was issued by the court in December 2008.

My story gets darker, though. The divorce left me in emotional ruin. I was alone and weak. I was vulnerable and bankrupt from the weight of it all. I could not process the nightmare and that cost me my life for a time.

PART VI

THE RABBIT HOLE

Darkness found me following the farewell to my children that February night and I returned to my apartment and stared outside the living room window. I remember thinking of the East River, knowing the turbulent river was moments way from where I sat. Every part of me wanted to take that plunge. *Why not? What is the point?*

I got off the chair and aimlessly paced the apartment. I found myself at the entrance of my kids' bedroom, staring at their beds full of stuffed animals, and I imagined them waking up in the mornings and arriving at their bedroom and giving them hugs and kisses.

That farewell was the beginning of the end for me, and I wanted to die on that freezing night and I needed something that would kill that awful feeling. I gravitated toward what was familiar to me, and the white wolf appeared, moving my torn body effortlessly into the kitchen and urging me to grab a large bottle of vodka and I poured the clear liquid into a large glass until it overflowed.

I returned to the living room, sat down on a red chair, and drank it quickly. Then I returned to the kitchen, grabbed the bottle, sat back down, and poured one drink after another until I was blind drunk—so drunk I could barely stand. I crawled to my bed and slithered up the side, rolled over onto it, and passed out.

That exact moment was my entry point into the Rabbit Hole and the white wolf was in control and I liked it. The man walking out of my former home that night was not the same one who went into it.

~

Every time I drank, I could feel pieces of me leaving. I continued to drink until there was nothing left. And my world shifted.

My days were now scheduled around the drink, and I would wake up most mornings blurry from the night before and the first thing I would feel was a deep sense of paranoia.

And the random thoughts started their march toward my brain. *What did I do last night?* I could not recall; I remembered only flickers of the city I might have been to, random bits of conversation I had, faces vague, select moments revealing my compromised state. The credit card receipts, or the ones I managed not to lose along the way of my drunken tour, were the best clues to the events of the night.

To not shake and calm my mind was key and the hiding game was now in full throttle. And I believed I controlled my secret and paid no attention to anything, and I was kidding myself and out of control.

And I was empowered and the more I acted out the more I affirmed I was still alive. I remember being drunk and crossing busy main avenues and dancing with the speeding taxis. And there was one time that I danced across the street and could feel the wind of the cabs flying by me and one driver honking the horn and cursing me. My attitude was, "Fuck you, motherfucker, hit me!"

And my sense of reality was what I thought it should be at any given moment and I wanted to die and I did not have the guts to do it.

~

I remember one night discreetly entering a popular lounge bar in SoHo, all lit up. I was drunk and I was encased in a metal drum of formaldehyde floating through the joint and I was undetected, and I was always mindful of the staff and I discreetly went to the bar and my eyes were heavy-lidded with vodka and I ordered a drink and it was a martini.

And I stood there sipping my drink and my bleary drink laden eyes peered about the lounge area for a place to land and that evening Barry appeared on the other side chatting it up with a few girls. Barry was a fixture in these places, and I got to know him well during this lost period in my life.

He was an affable guy who knew everyone, and everyone knew him. Many times, after work, I would head to a bar for a drink, and while sitting there Barry would call me. He would always ask, "Where are you?" I would tell him my location and within ten minutes he would roll in the joint. I thought, *How is this guy always ten minutes away from where I am?* It was uncanny to me.

He was a real estate developer but never really did much *development*. "Hey, Maxwell," he would always say, invariably invoking some form of real estate vernacular. "Found a great piece of dirt today, we can make millions." Dirt being the real estate lingo for a property site or building. I never questioned him or took anything regarding his real estate ventures seriously. I listened and smiled. He was a party-mate, that is it, a great guy, and he knew where every party was at any given time. That is all I cared about.

I headed his way, negotiating my balance as I traversed the length of the lounge floor. As I made my way to Barry, I felt a sense of repulsion about myself. I was lost and instinctively knew that this façade I created was going to end horribly.

Upon my arrival I made a hard landing right between Barry and the girl he was chatting up. "What's up Barry?" He appeared stunned for a brief second and then laughed like hell and introduced me to his entourage. He was always with a group, usually a lot of women, a bit older though. He was a polite guy, who was never without his blue blazer with gold buttons, blue jeans, and shoes with no socks.

He had the strangest hair. It was always slicked back and appeared to have implanted cornrows, perfectly lined, that revealed his scalp with other parts of his head showing thin lines of hair strips thickly greased back. The hair strips appeared to be surgically implanted on his head. The shape of his head was odd and resembled from behind that of a strawberry slowly expanding outward up from his neck. His face was inviting but carried a ruddy, reddish complexion.

Barry had that bloated, shiny, slightly stunned appearance. His eyes were a flat gray and anytime he was asked a question that required some thought he would project a stunned look at you like a deer caught in headlights. He was very deft at dodging questions that got too personal.

He loved the Mark Hotel on the Upper East Side and recommended that we go there. It was his office. "Let's get out of here and head to the Mark!" Barry shouted excitedly.

"Absolutely, yes," I blithely offered back while sipping my drink that would rock from side to side with vodka periodically splashing over the rim onto the table. He pulled back his chair, stood up in delight, and bluntly stated to the group, ordering them., "Let's move people." I felt he was going home.

I forgot to pay the bill and left my credit card behind as we exited the lounge and poured ourselves into a taxi, "Uptown, please, sir. "Yes, the Mark Hotel, 77th Street and Madison Avenue," Barry said. Barry laughed as we sped off. He never carried cash and while he came from a real estate dynasty, he was a vagabond always moving from one apartment to another that would last for a few days or so. He appeared to be the black sheep of his family and his parents would give him a small allowance, just enough to get him by. That did not seem to bother him. I could tell he had been living this way for many years. He smelled sometimes.

We all poured ourselves out of the taxi and into the Mark. The Mark Hotel was a repository for middle aged women who would hang out at the small tables and position themselves on the tiny mushy, hairy chairs that were impossible to find a comfortable sitting position in.

These resting chairs carried a seventies' look consisting of shaggy white and big black polka dotted fabric that you would find in some cheap roadside hotel in Montana or another part of the Southwest. These awful looking 'bean bag' chairs were scattered throughout the bar area, low seats where you were required to peer straight up at the ceiling as the waiters, appearing like towers, would look down upon you and quickly scribble down your drink order.

Millionaire and sometimes billionaire men would constantly parade through this area, (on occasion a celebrity would cruise by too), briskly making their way to the back of this place to the Jean George dining room for an expensive dinner. Usually an entourage followed behind, consisting, most times, of pretty women and the occasional perfectly coiffed mysterious European-looking figure.

The bar area women consisted primarily of gold diggers and newly minted divorcees (or veteran divorcees who had been swinging the bat for many years) on the hunt for a new wallet to seize. This was the place. And I would watch these gussied up ladies, eyes darting about the lounge area, constantly fixing themselves, peering up every time they would detect the faint rumble of a crowd sauntering through the bar area and into the dining room, hoping to get noticed.

They liked Barry, mostly as a prop though, as their fishing lines extended far out beyond us in search of the big catch. These ladies would tire after a while and one by one would excuse themselves and head back to their dwellings in hopes that the following evening would be the one where all their dreams of catching that older, rich man would come true.

The Mark made a nice martini though. That was all I was really interested in anyway.

As the night rolled on, Barry and I would hit more places than you could count. Barry's phone was like a 'beeper' receiving constant alerts on where another party was happening and off we would go. "Maxwell, we got a great party to go to, and it's free," he would always say.

~

That evening Barry received an alert on his phone that gave him the precise location of this very *discreet* party that luckily for us was happening only a few blocks away from the Mark. It was late in the evening. Barry nodded. "Let's go."

When we arrived, we were escorted into this apartment that felt the size of a football field. The place was packed with all types of rich folk, women draped in expensive garb and dripping in more high-priced jewelry than you could imagine. Men adorned themselves in expensive suits thick gold and platinum watches were wrapped around their wrists. They looked like characters from, 'Masters of the Universe.'

We were the proletariat, unbeknownst to this 'money-dipped' Manhattan elitist crowd, but nobody really cared. I was starting to ramp up a bit and Barry knew it, he encouraged it.

I spotted a cluster of gay guys a few meters away, all huddled. Hands swooned high in the air, hugs, frequent pecks on the cheeks, and glasses of wine positioned high above their heads as they clung to each other noisily, chirping like little birds, beaks pointed upward with occasional loud bursts of laughter, their thin exposed frames lunging back in glee, enjoying the raucous impromptu gathering.

I confidently cruised their way and started to dance up a storm with one of these delicate birds, twirling and tossing him around as he howled wildly, and the table applauded. They all loved it and were very understanding of my drunken act. They never judged. They were entertained. I liked that.

And they were listeners. I picked up that they carried a lot of pain. We were pain-mates. They were kind to me, and happy despite the weight they were forced to endure.

That night lasted through the early morning hours. I slowly passed out and woke up the next morning on a sofa, my eyes tired and glazed. The last of the party goers aimlessly wandered the apartment like the land of the living dead, all strung out. Others were embroiled in incoherent conversation, speaking frantically whiffing lines of cocaine, and sniffling constantly, their fingers adjusting their noses, heads lifting back to avoid nose drippings from crawling down their face from all the cocaine stuffed up their nostrils. I thought, as I was lying on the sofa, *This place is like a high-end crack house.*

I left the building alone and was instantly struck by the dense summer heat and bright sunlight that blinded my eyes as I searched for a taxi to get me to work. I was a mess and still high as hell. On the way downtown to my office, I stopped at my gym, and took a long, hot shower to rid myself of the headache and party stench leaking from my pores.

~

Nights were all pretty much the same. I would go to a bar wherever that might be, usually starting out in Midtown somewhere and then up at the Mark or downtown, usually alone, or with Barry.

I had thousands of places to go to and the white wolf was strong and no drink could put him down. I knew so many of them and they knew me. I was a happy goner, hugging anything in front of me, including a streetlamp if it was staring at me.

I got pretty good at making friends with the doormen. That was important since they were the first line of entry. A green light from them was the test. That got me into the den, and then all bets were off: backflipping into the booze I went. The truth is, the city was full of drunks, white-collar workers looking for a respite from the stresses of their jobs, relationships, or whatever. They were on a mission, too. I was in good company. The best was when some of the girls would retire for the night, but there were sometimes one or two who wanted the circus to continue. *Yes*, I thought. *I have bandmates to continue with my concert of carnage. The night just got longer.*

~

And New York City was reduced to nothing, and it was cold, lonely, unforgiving, and foreign in an instant. And the streets, restaurants, bars, and people were unrecognizable. And the neighborhoods that offered so much were now desolate, and I was alone and a drifter wandering with no future in this metropolis.

Everywhere I went in the city was a reminder of what I had lost. And it became a ghost town and the sense of new beginnings and endless possibilities that were so palpable to me when I first moved to the city had vanished. I was lost among the buildings and the bucolic park that I once adored and took refuge in. It was like touring a crash site littered with corpses, unidentifiable, buried among the steel of the carnage that descended from the sky out of nowhere.

I would constantly recount the events that led up to this mess. Flickers of conversations with my former wife would come to mind. I wondered what she must have been feeling. Did she feel a sense of loss? Was her return to France the right solution for her? Was that her happiness, or was she taking her problems and simply relocating them to a different place?

Adam's suicide was the end for me. When he departed, her only reason to be in New York vanished with him and she wanted out of this country.

~

I thought of my friend, Malachy. I wondered how his life turned out. He lived in the city, but we had lost touch many years prior. We had gone our own separate ways. He simply vanished from my life.

The last time I saw Malachy was at my sister's wake. I remember Malachy kept to himself, while my other friends hung out in the kitchen. I remember seeing him alone, near the coffin, not saying anything. I would catch him staring at the coffin. He was standing there by himself. He was connected to a loss that was not his. He carried the same pain I did that day, without any exchange between us. It was as if it was his sister that lay there in that coffin. I remember that he never got too close to it, though. He was keeping enough distance.

We did not speak at all that day. I felt he wanted it that way. I did feel compassion, as he stood there gazing at the coffin. He was lost in thought, like he was in some sort of trance.

During those nights of carnage, I could have used his company and wisdom that I recalled so well in my younger years. After all those years that passed, I still longed for his presence. When I thought of him, I felt calm, despite the nights of sheer havoc that became my life. That strange inner connection we had still resonated within me. He was ever present in my mind during the lost times. I thought maybe he could grab me by the hand, extricate me from the pain I was in, and release me back to a time that felt like another life.

~

In retrospect, it took a lot of effort for me to extract myself from what became a comfortably numb environment. I managed to extricate myself from it all, though there were many relapses along the way; pain was coming back to take me down again.

It was hard work to get it right. I was forced to address concepts of self-love and remove pain from my lexicon. As my mind tricked me, I needed to trick my mind. I needed strength and found great comfort thinking about my mother.

I remember during a very hot summer day in New York my mother and I took Mary to the hospital. As it turned out her immune system was so compromised that the doctor told us that he needed to perform a lumbar puncture on her. We all went to a small room on the hospital floor to perform the procedure. I had no idea what the procedure would entail. I just followed along behind the doctor and my mother, who was carrying my sister. When we entered the room, I was met with tremendous heat. The room was windowless, and I felt no air in there. It was horrible. My mom laid Mary down on a metal table that was very small and positioned in the middle of the room.

The doctor left and moments later he reappeared with a very long needle. It was scary looking. He instructed my mom and I to hold her down on her stomach since the procedure was extremely painful. We did and as the needle penetrated her lower lumbar area Mary let out the wildest shrieks. It was hard to hold her down since she took on this immense strength. The doctor insisted on us holding her down while he pushed the long needle into her back further and further. I was shaking and sweating during this whole thing. My mom was crying as she feebly soothed her daughter, bending over and whispering into her ear. I pleaded for the nightmare to go away.

~

And one night I confronted the white wolf at some after-hours downtown bar. The place was crowded, and I stood there holding the bar and the noise banged against my head and I longed for the tropical sea and the old man.

I moved into the bathroom and stared into the mirror and my face was disfigured and I saw the battle scars of the nights of carnage staring right back at me and my body was torn and frayed from the nights of loss.

And I thought to myself, *Who am I*...

I raced out and tumbled into a cab and rolled my tired body onto the dark and stained rubber seat and asked the driver to take me to Central Park. I was overwhelmed with a sense of doom peering up at the lights of the city, flickering through the window of the taxi as I raced toward the reservoir entrance on 80th and Fifth Avenue. As we neared the park, I could see the sun breaking and the dawn now upon me.

The driver was a nice man and although I could not see his face, he knew I was distraught and asked me if I was okay. "Sir, is everything all right? You are upset," he said.

I remained quiet but after a few moments replied, "I know, it's all too much, too much…"

He kept driving and then in a tender voice replied in broken English, "You will never find happiness in those places. They will lead you nowhere." I thought about his kind words and agreed with him.

We kept moving toward the park and when we arrived, I sat up to pay the driver. I saw several pictures of his children pasted to the dashboard and holy beads hanging from his rear-view mirror. I paid the fare and as I was exiting the taxi he calmly said, "Get some rest. You will feel better and just take care of you. Then, my friend, you will find peace."

I thanked him as I studied the pictures of his kids and said as I was leaving, "Your children are beautiful." He looked at me, smiled and then drove off and I saw the white wolf slowly vanish into the night. I wanted to be healed and I thought of my youth and Johnny and many great characters seared with this scar.

I walked to the reservoir in search of the old man. I wanted to talk to him and when I arrived, I saw a picture of the old man tacked to the water pump station façade and as I moved closer my ocean receded and I left.

I thought of Malachy…

PART VII

THE BENCH

Not long after my parole from the rabbit hole, I rekindle my relationship with Malachy. We meet in Central Park on a Saturday to sit down on an old green bench and talk.

On that hot and humid summer afternoon, the heat wave in New York City persists into its ninth day, and the heat index is over 104 degrees. The skyline is barely visible due to the oppressive humidity and sweltering conditions in the city.

I arrive at the park and enter using the east side 72nd Street access. Despite the oppressive conditions, the park is full of people: runners of all ages, shapes, and sizes, heading in all directions; the young and the old everywhere, with kids scurrying about as their parents keep a close eye on them. Long lines of folks bracing against the heat and humidity, eager to buy cold water and ice cream for themselves and their kids.

I hear faint music coming from the various performing stages that adorned that area of the park.

Bike riders in packs, with heads down and helmets on, tight spandex gear gripping their sweaty, overheated bodies, advance perfectly aligned along the undulating six-mile perimeter stretch of the park's famous loop that circles its entirety.

To my left as I enter the park is the familiar large playground where I would bring my kids. It is the largest children's playground in Central Park and crowded all the time. That day, the playground is overflowing with children playing on the swings, racing to the large sliding board, or jockeying for position to play in the sandbox, toys all over the place. Their parents sit on the benches precisely positioned around the playground, talking with friends while keeping a close eye on their kids.

I descend the steep incline toward the boathouse area that butts against Fifth Avenue. In the distance I see the green bench—that old green bench where I would sit and watch my kids play. There is the small lake in front of the bench, model sailboats cutting through the shallow green water, the hot summer breeze blowing those little boats in all directions.

I breathe slowly, listening to my cadence as I approach the bench. I think of my son. He is twenty-three years old now. He loved sailing the boats as a child. Flickering images of my girls race through my mind as I imagine them running to the Alice in Wonderland bronze statue. It is a few meters north of the lake. I remembered how excited they were, playing on that large bronze figure.

This old green bench faces the West Side skyline, and I see in the distance the pre-war buildings that line Central Park West. I catch a glimpse of the Dakota, a nineteenth-century Gothic-style structure, a mysterious, iconic dwelling where rumors of hauntings persisted over the centuries. I think of Roman Polanski's foreboding shot of the top of the building, the camera slowly descending onto the structure. That shot opens the film *Rosemary's Baby*. The Dakota morphed in an instant into something evil.

As I make my way to the bench, I study the multitudes of oak trees, lined up and lush, their green leaves bursting from the gangly branches. I imagine the author Lewis Carroll perched over there with Alice, his iconic creation, not far away.

I arrive, and there is Malachy sitting with a cup of coffee in his hand, staring across the lake. I see his thin frame, older now, his clothes falling off him, and a book in hand. His black rubber shoes firmly planted on the ground. His hair is still long, now grayish in color, tied back in a tight ponytail. He reminds me of an old professor sitting there as I approach him.

It is strange to reconnect with him after all the years. I see as I draw closer that he is negotiating the unrelenting heat and humidity, as he is fanning himself with his thick book and wiping the sweat off his brow. I study his profile and see the young kid I knew so many years back and the sight of him gives me a warm feeling. I am sure that that thick book is a Russian literature piece, since that is all he would read when we were younger. That and comic books.

Malachy turns his head to the left and peers up at me, our eyes meeting for the first time in decades. He slowly gets up from the bench, trying not to spill his coffee. I see as he reaches out to shake my hand that he is nervous. He fidgets with his book, his long, thin body shifting back and forth. His eyes still maintain a youthful quality, those piercing blue eyes that see right through me.

Malachy is a shy person to begin with, and this meeting after all this time must be awkward for him.

I don't' know what to expect and just go with the flow. I am nervous too.

"I hope you're comfortable here," I say. "We even have a little shade today, and a slight breeze. I like it here."

He nods, offering an unnatural response. He clears his throat. "It's nice here, Maxwell. I think it's good you chose this place. It calms the mind."

I think of a play he once spoke of. I guess the bench reminds me of it. "Malachy, you remember the play that took place in the park. What was it? Oh, yes, *The Zoo Story*. A bench was the central prop in that one-act play, and Edward Albee wrote it, right? I believe I read it a long time ago. When we were young, you told me you liked the fact that it all took place in the park, on a bench, and you liked those two characters who met there."

He grins slightly. He seems more relaxed. "Yes, I remember. Albee wrote it in three weeks."

I'm surprised. I mean, I never thought anyone, especially some famous playwright, could come up with a story like that so fast. "I didn't know that. Wow, that's incredible."

He takes a sip of his coffee and continues to stare out over the lake. He is having some trouble making direct eye contact with me. "So, Maxwell, how are things with you?"

I don't know where to begin or what to say. I had just gotten released out of my own private perdition. I feel embarrassed, I'm still trying to process it all. "Well, Malachy, there are a lot of things that didn't turn out the way I expected, that's for sure."

I ask him how he is doing, but he deflects my question. I could tell he wants to keep the conversation focused on my life. When we were kids, he never liked to focus on himself unless he was talking about books or movies that he liked. When it came to his personal life, he would recoil when I asked him anything about it.

He thinks for a moment before speaking. "Well, wow, I hope you're okay. I mean, you seem well. I know it's been a long, long time, but those days when we were kids I'll always remember. They were great times we spent together. I often reflect on those moments. When

I was coming over here, I was thinking about your dad. He was a funny guy, carried a lot of that guilt stuff. I was thinking of all those times he would make you angry to no end with those guilt trips, like going to church. You would lie to him all the time about going. Remember when he would quiz you on the homily, for Christ's sake, and if you got it wrong, which you always did, he would nail you on it. You remember that stuff?"

"Yes, I do," I say.

Silence then ensues and Malachy looks away and stares out over the lake.

I go further, as his silence is killing me. "You knew my pop, Malachy. You could only take it so far with him. When opinions were introduced, the dialogue got lost, and judgment was invited into the room. I guess that was the way it was."

Malachy awakens. "I remember him that way. He was a character, speaking with that pipe hanging out of his mouth that he would light fifty thousand times. The thing kept going out."

"Yeah. He had a lot of pipes but had no idea how to smoke them. In hindsight though, I believe many in my family could only take it so far, and with age, those walls or limitations grew that much more. So, I told myself to 'forget this' and started to drift, slowly."

Malachy makes a thoughtful observation. "Perhaps your drifting was a way to bring order into your life against the chaos you saw all around you."

I had never thought of it that way. "I agree, Malachy."

I'm surprised that we are going this deep after so many years apart. A part of me, though, wants to.

Malachy then gets right to the point. "Are you feeling guilty, Maxwell? I'm smelling that guilt thing sneaking in the back door, my friend."

I don't' want it to appear to him that I'm bashing my dad. It was a long time ago. I nervously blurt out, "When I think about it, though, maybe I overlooked the reasons that led him down his own path. Perhaps I ignored his pain. I mean, he did raise me, put a roof over my head, fed me, educated me, and I still wanted more. Maybe he wasn't capable of being intimate or showing love the way, I expected."

Malachy listens as he tousles his long ponytail in thought. "Okay, so he did his job. You're a dad. You're doing yours too. You're much older now, and he continues to take your mind hostage. I told you this when we were kids. You ignored me. You let him make you feel guilty. "

"Okay, got it. Please hear me out though."

Malachy leans back, ready to listen.

I let go. "I mean, he endured a caustic and unforgiving mother. He never talked about his father. He was an only child. He had no one to talk to, to confide in. That must have been a very lonely place for a child." I stop and look at Malachy. I am rambling now.

Malachy motions for me to continue.

So I do. "I mean, he wanted to impress his mother. Appearances were important to him. He joined the priesthood, only to abruptly leave. Why? I'll never know, but I was told that his decision was met with harsh judgment by the community. His mother wouldn't talk to him. Friends were suspicious of his vocation, given the war that passed him by. That must have really hurt. Perhaps his world as a young man was a broken place."

Malachy hesitates for a second and then responds. "Maxwell, like you, maybe he felt too much judgement in his life and ran from it. The guy only revealed himself to strangers. Why was that? You get it. You can't let go… really. Listen to yourself."

I respond. "I'll say this, Malachy. Maybe he wasn't loved the way he desired as a child or a young adult and couldn't express those feelings toward others, since he was left without them himself."

Malachy pushes back and then says, "Okay, but why do you continue to carry this burden with you, this weight?" Malachy continues. "You might be right about his fears of not being good enough and that he ran in fear of being judged himself. He wore it on his sleeve but whacked you if he felt you were onto him."

Malachy pauses, thinking, as his fingers stroke his ponytail. "Maybe your subconscious is trying to wake you up. The things you're disclosing tap into your essence. I believe they play a central role in some of the guilt you carry today." He pauses again. "Let's talk about your guilt. You okay with that? How do you see it? Can you go there?"

I am silent. I have no idea how to respond.

Malachy then asks, "Maxwell, what does guilt mean to you?"

"To be honest, I still can't get my head around it. Maybe it's that Catholic guilt. It's all about control. I believe that. A weaponized thing that appears uninvited and out of nowhere. When we were kids, you were made to feel it. It was never said to you that you should feel guilty. It was this unsaid thing. It was in the air, and you were forced to inhale it, or it would inhale you. You know what I mean?"

Malachy shoots right back at me, "Maxwell, the goal is to reduce the duality that is battling in your mind. Guilt! You're not going to rid yourself of it if the subconscious still knows it." He then asks me a question unrelated to my father. "Do you feel guilty about your kids leaving?"

I draw in a breath and heave it out in a sigh. "Not a day goes by that I don't think about it."

"Is that guilt you're feeling, Maxwell, or is it something else?" He pauses again. "Think about it. This bench that you chose gives you joy. Then, in an instant, it becomes a place of pain. Why is that? Is this place really a reminder of all that you lost? Why can't it be a place where you can capture something positive? Your kids played here. That should conjure up positive memories in you, not guilt."

I retort back, "I have trouble looking at it that way. I don't know why."

Malachy quickly responds, "The guilt will slow down only when you can fully express how it planted its roots in your subconscious in the first place."

"That's hard for me to respond to. I hear it, but to tell you how it got there in the first place is difficult for me. Maybe guilt came into my subconscious at an early age, like when I was a child. Maybe it took root then and never left."

Malachy nods. "When will this end for you, so that you can love yourself and start living? Come on, your dad is dead. Let him go! Your relationship with your kids is great. They're older now. They love you. So why allow guilt to mess that up?" He wipes his brow again, looking out over the lake, and speaks without making any eye contact with me. "More to my point, Maxwell, is this guilt you're living with, or is it something else?"

I think for moment. "Like I said, I drag the past into the present. I constantly see my kids as the children they were when they left years ago. They're becoming adults now."

Malachy becomes agitated with my response. "Your kids aren't thinking that way. *You* are!"

Malachy takes a deep breath and asks if he could be alone for a minute or two. I comply and lift myself off the bench and walk a few feet toward the lake, watching those little boats swirling around.

A few minutes pass, and Malachy asks me to come back to the bench.

He opens with an observation. "That mess, as you call it, your lunge into the drink to quell the pain, may have been the biggest blessing you'll ever receive. It taught you, whether you're aware of it or not, to love yourself. Otherwise, you would still be there, in that dark place. It offered you a rebirth. Be grateful for that. The irony of it all is that what you thought you lost was never really lost. Your kids never really left. You just didn't see it. *You* checked out, not *them*. They're not blaming you for that. Guilt and pain can do a lot of damage. You get that?"

I remain silent.

Malachy slowly gets up from the bench and turns his back toward me. He stands there facing the lake for what seems to be an eternity. He then turns and slowly sits back down. He remains silent for a minute, staring out over the lake, lost in thought.

Finally he turns back toward me and asks a simple question. "Do you think the guilt you feel and have been feeling for so many years is really something else?"

I had no idea what he was talking about. *Something else?*

Malachy looks me straight in the eye, and bluntly says, "Maxwell, are we talking about guilt here, or really your anger—your anger at those you believe to be responsible for your pain? Collette, right? She took the kids to France. She didn't want to co-parent. She stuck lawyers in the middle of your divorce. She kept a secret from you. That secret could have been avoided with the truth of it all. You love your daughter and only wanted the best for her whatever the truth was. She told you she fell out of love with you. In your mind, her actions toward you left you with nothing, left you lost, a worthless human—alone, broke and finished. Right?"

He continues, "While I am saying the truth of what happened to you the question becomes what got you both to that point. Did you ever consider that she might have been angry at you. And if you both have no inner peace, how are you both going to find it outside of yourselves; surely not with each other. Think of the word "harmony", what does that word mean to you?

I remain quiet.

He does not stop. Well, when your instrument – you—are surrounded by discordance and you find yourself in disharmony, or worse taking this disturbance to levels of fear, anger and contempt, you are out of balance, out of harmony and you should acknowledge it instead of indulging in it, or worse blaming yourself or justifying it. Did you ever stop to think that you both were out of tune, and that state of being would preclude you finding inner peace or a connection with each other. Thus, anger eventuates, logical right?! Remember anger is a direct manifestation of what you couldn't find a way to deal with, that disharmony within, that raging unresolved internal conflict that has been residing in your subconscious. Your father too. Come on. You respected him but deemed yourself guilty for his unhappiness, not yours."

I put my head down, hands covering my eyes.

Malachy doesn't' stop there. "Maxwell, we're not finished yet "We have one more thing that's very important to talk about."

"What?" I ask.

He responds in a low tone. "Self-love and forgiveness." He asks if I am okay with continuing.

I say yes and listen.

"Now that you know it was never guilt that led to your trip into the abyss but instead the anger and eventuating pain that got you there, now you need to ask yourself a simple question."

I wait.

"That is, 'How do I begin to reconcile this anger and *be in harmony...,* resolve the internal conflict that exists within me?' That will be your release, your joyful state of mind for you to reclaim. That's your path toward meaning in your life and an end to the turmoil that got you into the abyss. Self-love is another way to say, 'I honor myself.' It's an affirmation of your worth as an individual, as a human. Now, once you attain that self-love and work on keeping it as a part of you, then you can forgive others, including your former wife and your father." Remember Maxwell, it is not we who make the path; it is we who give it direction. This is our true power. Perhaps my friend the world has no meaning at all—it is a gift from Him to us to discover one.

He is right, and the relief is overwhelming. I lose myself for a moment and don't' know where I am.

~

I am running in the park. The ocean is beneath my feet. My endorphins are exploding. The sun is awakening.

Epilogue

I never came face to face with a hurricane as a child or young adult. These acts of Mother Nature are mesmerizing. I thought these extreme storms were a product of some arbitrary freakish weather assault that would offer me a feeling of heightened reality; something to watch from a distance, an event I relegated to some form of live entertainment. I mean, the concept of the 'hurricane party' is pretty much an affirmation of what I and most others believe about these astounding, unpredictable events that come our way each year. We treat these extreme storm events like some sort of circus act, there to watch and please us as audience members, rarely, if ever, venturing into anything beyond the name we ascribe to it, in this case Hurricane Irma.

That viewpoint I had carried with me changed later in life when Irma unexpectedly arrived at my doorstep. She taught me that there is something out there much bigger than me, divine in nature, and put into perspective the cataclysmic, life altering changes, like a hurricane, that can appear in life.

As I reflected on the events of that hurricane that I was for the first time a part of and that persisted for more than twenty hours with unrelenting force and unpredictability, I felt throughout this experience her sheer force; divine in nature that is not of our creation and had arrived to teach me something, perhaps about myself.

~

The night of her arrival, she became my unexpected and new teacher. Her relentless banging against my building, windows, and doors, and my mind forcing herself into my being, she instructed me to explore on a deeper level how important it is to practice gratitude and humility not just in good times but when times in my life are at the lowest. She was extremely erudite and made clear to me that the lowest moments are the times when my gratitude and humility need to be ever more present in my mind.

Irma was my teacher. She was to be a super hurricane, set to make landfall on September 10, 2017, and projected to engulf South Florida. She moved slowly, which only heightened concerns, like how long this teacher would force us to remain in the classroom before letting us out— hopefully without injury. She was a ruthless but truthful teacher that had no interest in pleasing her pupils; she was only there to force her class to take a second, harder, more considered look at themselves and their behavior.

As she loomed out there in the sea waiting to strike, I could feel her presence more and more with each passing hour prior to her arrival. She was getting front and center attention in the news media around the world. She was the star that dominated the national conversation. Everyone thought of her constantly, hoping and praying that she would be kind enough to spare them from losing their homes and lives.

Irma did not respond to their pleas but instead methodically continued her march toward the shores of Florida. She played with us as she made her way toward our southern shores. She would turn a little this way or that way, forcing us to adjust the red zones, the places where she would directly hit us. She kept us on our toes, intentionally.

Panic and fear engulfed her students as food stores were now packed. She liked that; a sobering reality and awakening for her students, she thought, was to be an important part of her lesson. Water and canned food, usually ignored by us, suddenly became hot commodities; her students now frantically grabbing whatever they could find and as much as possible, to ensure they would not be left without the necessities.

She laughed when she thought, *canned food and water, what! Those commodities are something my pupils never dwelled on, for they were to be expected. Why now? I must be scaring them. That's a good thing. It balances the mind and spirit.* She thought, *this is*

necessary for my lesson to resonate, students with clear
heads, focused on my arrival and teachings.

I thought how crazy it was to see how we students in an instant can go from feelings of total complacency, perceived notions of infallibility, operating our lives in the way we desire (that is in our absolute control) to an immediate loss of control, to panic and fear. Our conceited belief that nothing can permeate the perceived reality that we hold intact, that we confidently protect against any outside intruders.

This is us, yes, pacing those same stores, daily, with a total sense of ease and comfort and in total control of our surroundings and choices to then see our acquired microcosm instantly shatter and shift from comfort to desperate survival in an instant.

~

While Irma was stressful, as I did not know what to anticipate, her impending arrival also felt exhilarating; a sense of the unknown, and new heightened reality swept through me. I received a barrage of calls from family and friends demanding that I evacuate. I ignored them since it was too late as far as I was concerned. She was too close now.

No flights were coming into Florida, and few if any flights were quickly leaving the State. So, I thought, what was the point? It would be a mess, and I would be stuck at the airport for who knew how long. I concluded the best place to be was right where I was, twenty-four stories up with a bird's eye view of this impending goliath.

I got one call only a day or so from landfall, in which I was told I had a death wish. This person, who is my sister, Maggie, threatened that she was coming to Florida to get me and fly me back to New York City. The conversation was funny. I retorted, "Even if you make it here, we will not be flying anywhere but rather throwing our own hurricane party."

Other callers were more interested in what the local news reports were saying and where I was physically located in her path. When I explained that I was on the beach in the red zone, I could feel the callers were stunned that I would take such a chance. Severe weather events scare the hell out of most people. The media, I believe, takes full advantage of escalating those fears.

~

Leading up to her arrival, the building was quickly evacuating. I would spend most of my time with the doorman, watching the condo inhabitants nervously dragging their luggage through the lobby and into the taxis and car services that were lined up out front. They were scared and had no interest in taking any chances with the unpredictable nature of hers.

The doorman was a local resident of the Miami area. He was a young, affable guy, who witnessed these extraordinary acts of nature and educated me on the realities of her impending visit which was only several hours away.

He explained that pretty much the entire building had evacuated since their biggest concern was direct damage to their unit and being stuck without food or water if the damage was what the meteorologists were predicting. Some older folks had concerns with access to medical care.

He told me that I was the only person in the building that decided to stay. I asked him if he thought my move was foolish and he said no. He explained that it was already too late to get a flight out of Florida despite the reports still maintaining that there was a window of opportunity to leave the State. He told me that Irma could be something new, though; a super storm that could be unprecedented and exact a lot of carnage.

He advised me that if things got tricky there was a 'bomb hurricane shelter' under the building and that the engineer would get me there. "However," he said, "if it comes to that, you will need to walk down the twenty-four flights and have some food since that type of hit could keep us all stuck in that bunker in the aftermath of this event for quite a while."

So, I was left with a few workers who stayed on to ensure the security of the high-rise, an engineer, and my nice doorman. The workers were interesting to watch. I knew some of them. They were at it all day and every day, feverishly erecting steel panels in advance of

Irma's arrival. They rapidly prepared for her land fall, slamming up steel panels across the entire cylinder-shaped building, removing every object that had the potential to become airborne, and everything else imaginable to secure the safety of the building. Some workers would talk to me as they attended to their tasks, asking why I was still here. I told them it was too late to get out. They laughed and I could tell they thought my decision to stay was dangerous.

~

The day Irma was scheduled to hit the southern coast the weather was gorgeous, the ocean a flickering green and blue with larger surf than usual. I decided to go for a swim, and it was delightful. The ocean had a different feel, with strong currents under the surface. I could see rip currents forming all around me.

The rip currents are easy to spot. They appear out of nowhere and take on a sandy brown color, churning up the sand on the ocean bottom with little white caps and peeling back with force out to sea and dissipate. The key with an undertide if you get caught in one is to never fight against its direction. Most people who do fight this type of riptide get tired very quickly and begin to panic which is no good. A rip while pulling you out to sea also pushes you down under the water which can drown a person. It is critical that you allow the rip current to do its thing, keep your head above the water and let it take you out to sea and drop you off.

I also noticed the dark and low puffy clouds taking shape off the coast. I swam for a long time and the warm water with its cross currents were fun to navigate. During those moments I felt at peace and exhilarated. I was totally alone which was an added pleasure and gave me a sense of myself; a tactile feeling that is indescribable, emoting a sense of euphoria. Perhaps it comes from being in the grasp of something bigger than myself and totally unpredictable. My senses were on fire.

I got caught in one rip current that dragged me almost to the dark blue water, or the no man's zone, as I called it. The light green almost aqua water suddenly turned into a dark blue opaque ocean where you had no depth or sight into the water, like the North Atlantic. While I was not concerned about the riptide at this point, I was concerned about the sharks, since with storms of this nature, this heavily churned up sea causes sharks and other sea life to get confused. As a result, they get lost and move closer to shore. In the case of sharks, they also become more agitated with the confusion and are more aggressive with other sea life, including humans if they are in the way.

Plus, I knew that the distance I was offshore would take a while for me to reach shoreline given the cross currents and general aggressiveness of the ocean as I could feel it picking up strength very quickly as I began my journey back to the shore.

I pushed hard and made it back, a mile or so to the north of my beach, given the currents that swept me along the coast, but I was happy to now be firmly planted on shore. I walked back to the condo. The sojourn was enjoyable as well.

As I trekked back, I studied the horizon and saw the black clouds looming, portentous of the events to come and rapidly moving closer to the shore. I could also feel the rings, the hurricane rain bands, begin to come down, moving sideways with periodic blasts of warm air that would push me a little bit.

I knew Irma was flexing her muscles and nearing her students. It gave me such a thrill to be alone with her. It was spiritual to me. I felt at one with her and looked forward to meeting her later that night. She was strong.

~

The weather newscasts were dire in their assessment of Irma, her strength that we would come to know in a few hours. With each news report, the situation only got worse. She clearly intended that. I heard everything: that this would be the storm of the century; that winds would reach force five, more than a hundred and sixty miles per hour. Mandatory evacuation was imperative for all those residents in her path. I remained right in the sweet spot of the red zone of her path.

As darkness took hold and the sea looked jet black, the phone calls that pounded my ears earlier now went silent. I guess the worried folks gave up and went back to their routine with an eye on her. I took my last trip to the lobby that was now quiet. All the tenants had left, and the workers were gone. It was the doorman, me, and the engineer, alone in that lobby. We spoke for a while. I grabbed the engineer's cell phone number and took my last elevator ride back up to my condo.

~

The night ensued and it was black as black can be. I could not see the water now. The rain and wind became constant since the inner bands of her were almost upon me. This was her teaser since it would not be until almost dawn that her full force would arrive to greet me.

That night was a meditation for me and a time where I did a lot of reflection. Although I was alone and isolated with burning candles all around me, since while the power was still working it would sometimes go off and on depending on the wind and rain, I felt a peace that allowed me space. My mind was quiet, I felt bliss.

My thoughts were random but spiritual and positive in nature. I thought about my youth, my children, those that departed and those still walking this planet. I felt a great degree of gratitude and humility sitting among the flicker of those candles alone, listening to her hard driving rains and ferocious gusts outside that night.

The silence in my dwelling was peaceful against the wild cacophony outside; it was to me a sign that my spirit was settled, my life reborn, my self-love absolute and all the restlessness of my being now residing outside of me, in the hands of my teacher who allowed my internal reconciliation to be undisturbed, pure and quiet. She took away the tremors I internalized for much of my life and made them her own; she became my protector and I was grateful for her compassion.

She continued to remain very close to me as her winds around midnight began gusting heavily at probably one hundred and twenty-five plus miles per hour. The night was long with constant bursts of her slamming against everything in her way. She was only moments away.

~

Irma finally arrived and she was amazing to watch. She was beautiful. I felt no fear. I felt peace.

I observed her during this onslaught, witnessing her gusts of winds reach over one hundred and forty-five miles per hour as she swept out of the southeast and around the building. She was fierce but very agile.

I could stand on the balcony since her winds were sweeping around my side of the building and trailed through a narrow path between my building and the building next door. It was like standing next to a jet plane engine as the plane took off. The noise was relentless and loud as hell. My hair stood on end as I witnessed ferocious winds of her spin past me. I was in awe of this gorgeous woman.

We lost power only to regain it and lose it again. The tidal surges she created were amazing to view. The water retracted several hundred meters, only to then surge forward, smashing against the building. She was determined and relentless, flexing her muscles.

The poor folks who scattered to the local airports, Miami International and Fort Lauderdale, were stuck there for almost a week. There were water shortages and overcrowding. I heard it was a nightmare for those people. There was no way to get back to Miami Beach, since there were no taxis, and even if there were, Miami Beach was closed. Those who fled were unable to return for almost a week. It got a little freaky for me at night and into the early morning hours, with candles burning and the cacophony. There was no difference between day and night; it all was one.

Unrelenting noise and driving rain that was like piercing bullets persisted for almost twenty hours without a break. I could hear heavy debris flying like missiles crashing into the side of the building. She was tireless, so I thought.

~

When she finally departed, I left the building to see the carnage she left as a reminder: stores razed, glass all over the place, sand piled up on the streets, electrical lines scattered about, and hordes of engineers, police, and firefighters working around the clock to piece this mess back together. I was without any power that day and for several days thereafter the power would come and go. The building, I was told, suffered a lot of structural damage.

The beach was almost gone as the ocean captured most of it. There were all kinds of debris scattered everywhere along the shoreline. The ocean, while appearing a bit calmer, still had a threatening quality to it. The waves were still large, and the remaining winds would peel against their faces, creating tremendous ocean sprays that would lift off the tops of waves and into the blue sky.

I was out of food and my water supply was slowly depleting. No stores were open. Rather, most were boarded up, and many were leveled. I asked a cop if there was anything open and he simply nodded his head with a shrug. I continued south on Collins Avenue, looking at the carnage all around me, careful not to step on an electrical wire.

Miraculously, while searching for water and food, I saw a small, elderly man carrying two plastic bags that appeared to look like bags with food in them. I immediately raced over to him. He was Russian and could barely utter a word in English. He explained where I could cop something to eat. A small Russian market was open a few blocks down the main street, Collins Avenue.

I sped over there. While it was crowded with Russians, I managed to buy food and water. I got my wish, a bit later in life, but it came in any event. The whole experience was absolutely exhilarating to me. I will never forget it and I thank her for the moments we shared together. She was a great teacher.